CELLING

YOUR

SOUL

CELLING YOUR SOUL

No App for Life

Joni Siani

ISBN: 978-1492384007

Credits

Book Editor: Elizabeth Good

Cover: Design by WeAreMoore.com/Nandor Moore

Siani Scale, p. 205: WeAreMoore.com/Nandor Moore
        Photography: Jimmy Ji
        Model: Ben Abbene

Siani Steps, p. 211: CPorterDesigns.com/Coni Porter

To Morgan,

The best human being on the planet....

I love you with all my heart

...and to the depth of my soul.

In the spirit of our ever-declining attention span...

Conclusion

"Everything's Amazing and Nobody's Happy"
— Louis CK

We have been enthralled and dazzled by our amazing digital world, awed by the boundless connections we can make with one another, wowed by the celebrity-like attention we can get in an instant from a post or tweet. But as amazing as our technology is, it cannot feed our soul and our spirit, and that's why we are feeling like crap.

Celling Your Soul explains some of the reasons why we have allowed ourselves to be so socially dependent on our cell phones and gadgets of the 21st century. It examines the psychological and physiological effects that our 24/7 connections have had on an entire generation. The goal here is to gain a better understanding of ourselves, our relationships, and the world around us, and how we can best incorporate our 21st century digital technology into our human experience in order to enrich our lives. It is time for us to reevaluate our priorities so that technology is serving us, rather than us serving technology.

Success can be defined as meeting the goal of our ambitions. In order for us to make that determination, we must clearly define our objectives. So, what exactly is the goal of our contemporary communication and information technology? We were promised technological advances with devices that would make us *smarter* and *more social*, enrich our relationships, bring us closer, make us feel safer and more secure, and make life easier. Have these things happened?

The devices of the 21st century *are* fulfilling the communication objective in regard to efficiency in the *delivery* of messages at lightning speed, from person to person, en masse, and without any restrictions. They have become a source of infinite daily information, a platform for products and services such as the world has never seen.

They *have* allowed every individual the opportunity to be seen and heard by every other person on the planet 24 hours a day, seven days a week, 365 days a year. They *have* given every one of us the freedom and opportunity to express our thoughts, opinions, talents, and images.

However, these devices have *also* caused us to isolate and disconnect ourselves from one another on an emotional and personal level. They are being overused and are creating compulsive, addictive, insensitive, dependent, impulsive, and self-centered behavior. They are also creating confusion and unrealistic expectations that are negatively affecting our personal development, relationships, and mental well-being. Contrary to intentions, they are *not improving* our **personal** communication and social skills within the objective of deepening our connections or understanding of one another.

> *"The world's economic superpower, the United States,*
> *has achieved striking economic and technological progress over*
> *the past half century without gains in the self-reported*
> *happiness of the citizenry."*
> World Happiness Report, *Columbia University, 2012*

Statistically, we are not happy, and we're not sure what we can do about it. Technological innovators have misrepresented the capabilities of these devices in order to make billions of dollars. We have come to believe that we must have them in order to fulfill our human and personal needs. The communication options that we have today are simply being misused. The problem is not the devices, but the devices in the hands of operators who are depending on the devices to do the work of "connecting" for them. For many people, the devices are not being used to bring us together for enriching our personal and emotional connections in a way that fulfills our spirit and soul.

FOCUS ON A SOLUTION

Research is now emerging that supports what we have been seeing and fearing for a long time. However, exposure to a problem is only the beginning. It's important to move to the next step and propose some long overdue corrections to the issues of our digital world.

First, we need a priority shift. Our fascination with technology seems to have distorted our priorities within the connection process. We must value people over gadgets and devices. Technology has a place in our 21st-century society when it is used properly, but not at the **expense** of devaluing authentic and personal connections.

Second, we must understand *ourselves* within the human experience. We are not machines. The communication process for human connection and relations is complex and must be respected beyond the scope of the exchange of data. The focus must return to the development of our social and communication skills in order to fulfill the deeper level of connectivity we need in our daily lives.

Finally, we need to follow a protocol for *using* our digital devices within a value system where our personal communication and social skills are cultivated and enhanced and where social civility, news integrity, and basic humanity are the *priority* over speed and fascinating gadgetry.

Three simple steps to start, that's all...

Dedication

This book is dedicated to my students. During countless discussions on communication issues affecting those born and raised in the digital world, referred to as the "iGeneration," "Millennials," "Generation Screwed," or the "hook-up nation," you strongly urged me to "share" some of the strategies, information, and exercises dedicated to changing perspective and improving personal communication, social skills, and values in our human relations that have made a positive impact on your life.

In the world of technology, your generation has been vulnerable participants in a global social science experiment. We are just now feeling the unintended fallout. Thank you for sharing your emotional and honest feelings during this most interesting time in our technological history. During our many face-to-face conversations and small group discussions, we were reminded of the simple power each one of us possesses when we learn to value one another.

Your honesty about how you really feel about the world we live in continues to allow others to understand that they're not alone, and actually "not crazy." We learned the benefits of patience, and how devoting a little more time to authentic communication can lead to more enriching human connections in a world of digital over-connectivity.

You are the generation that will be responsible for "pulling the plug" on members of my generation, so it's important to improve social skills in the way of compassion, empathy, and other human apps that might be lost in our digital world. (Smiley Face!)

Contents

Chapter 1

Generation Screwed

In July 2012, Joel Kotkim of *Newsweek* magazine wrote an article, called "Generation Screwed," explaining that the baby boomer generation had inherited a thriving economy. However, a combination of "greed, shortsightedness and blind partisanship" virtually set up a world for the next generation that fuels unemployment, a major wealth gap, and greater college debt than we've ever seen, just to have young people graduate and then move back into their parents' homes.

The "boomers" who were graduating and launching their careers and adult lives in the "greed is good" economic era of the 80s created a value shift far from the anti-materialism of the 60s and 70s. The children born to this generation, those born in the 80s and 90s, have become the first of the cradle-to-grave consumers in a sea of stuff. These are the children who have been raised with the parental value of *"the one with the most toys when they die, wins."* It has not served our society well, and as we look around at our economy, a burst housing bubble, and more debt than ever, it may be time for a thorough evaluation.

We are also living in what has officially become known as the "information age." What happens when you have technological advances in a world that values corporate bottom-line profits over the best interests of consumers? The gadgets, toys, and digital devices that have come into our lives as "must-have" items are being purchased as routinely as any basic household or personal item, because we have been conditioned to feel that we must have the latest and greatest "everything."

It is every generation's responsibility to think about the legacy they're leaving for the next generation. In other words, instead of being shortsighted and selfish, we're supposed to be thinking long-term and self*less*. However, it seems that shortsightedness has been our model for the past couple of decades. Invent, create a need, and people will buy. This system has been the economic cornerstone of our world for the past few decades.

Perhaps if we were doing great right now, we'd be able to say, "Well, I guess we can't argue with the system." But we're not. We're not doing great economically, we're not doing great socially, we're not doing great in physical health, and we're not doing great in mental well-being. We have produced a society that is more anxious and stressed-out than ever before. We are using more anti-anxiety, anti-depression, anti-ADHD, and anti-OCD medications than ever before. We are more disconnected emotionally, and that has contributed to our young adults being pretty miserable.

> *Incidence of depression has increased every year in the past century. People with depression frequently suffer from anxiety.*
> *University of Minnesota*

One factor that can no longer be ignored is the exponential growth of our digitally enhanced world. For all the promises of technological "advances" and communication devices that are supposed to make life better, we are clearly seeing the evidence of a few decades of shortsightedness, and even blindness, in the face of negative feedback from an industry that has generated billions and billions of dollars. We invented, we created a need, we purchased... and now we have to face the backlash.

> *In 2013, for the first time, the* Diagnostic and Statistical Manual of Mental Disorders, *or* DSM-V, *includes Internet Addiction Disorder as a "condition for further study."*

We have all either said to ourselves, or have heard others say jokingly, that we are "addicted" to our phones. We are freaked out by phantom vibrations from a phone that isn't there, we have compulsive feelings that we can't survive a day without our cell phones, and we have conditioned an entire society to obsessively and compulsively feel the need for nonstop "checking" for information updates. It has become routine for us to leave the house with wallet, keys, and phone — a routine that has become part of our culture in less than a decade. So, why this strange relationship with a piece of technology?

It's very simple. We are, at our very core, hardwired to connect with one another. We have always known that people need people. However, it has only been in the past decade that we have indoctrinated an entire generation to believe that they need a *device* in order to "connect." The mediated message and the digital revolution of endless products say "this is the *thing* you *need*" in order to *feel* connected. We dutifully responded overwhelmingly with getting the "thing"... and believing, "Now that I have the 'thing,' I will be 'connected' to other people."

Instead of being more connected to people, we have found ourselves more connected to the devices. What we forgot was to teach our kids how to connect emotionally, speak to be understood, empathize, listen, clarify, look, respect, give attention, focus, and do all those parts of the communication process that actually allow for the personal connections we need in order to thrive. The message that this generation received was that communication is mostly about the speed of the data exchange rather than about interpersonal communication skills.

LOVE, INTIMACY, SEX: PART 1

The promises of technology to help us connect came with some unforeseen consequences. The initial idea was theoretically positive: easier access to one another. However, being "on-call" for one another 24/7 either forced us to go crazy trying to keep up with the impossible demands, or turned us inward and away from each other into our own personal digital bubbles.

We've created a generation of young people starved for more opportunities for face-to-face bonding, yet feeling most comfortable reaching out to others through their thumbs. In addition to economic problems, including sky-rocketing college loans, another way that young adults have been screwed-over is in the misinformation and mediated misconceptions on how to communicate with one another in order to build and create fulfilling, meaningful, and authentic personal connections. Our technological advances have created some disadvantages in the way of social skill development that, as long as we are human, we will always need.

We human beings are social by nature. We are hardwired to connect to other human beings, to be in the physical presence of others, simply because that is how we are created. It is how we thrive. In order to meet the needs of our best human experiences, we need to communicate with one another.

Fundamentally, the primary function of human communication is to connect on a level that will keep the species going. For most animals, there is a sound, a call, a smell, or something that says "I'm ready!" For humans, in all cultures and time periods, we have created social behaviors and standard mating rituals that lead to emotional and physical "connections" that become the human experience. In my "era," I was passed a note with two options:

check Yes if you like me, or No if you don't. It was all pretty simple. No posting, blogging, or updating of status every five minutes.

Why do we find ourselves so attracted to one particular person? How do we explain the love-at-first-sight phenomenon, or at least lust at first sight? How do we explain this "chemistry" thing? And, how do we get that to happen to us? It is one of the great mysteries of the world. What we do know is that without that mysterious connection, the human species will no longer exist. *It*, whatever "it" is, continues to be the driving motivation for human "connections" emotionally, spiritually, developmentally, and sexually.

Is it any wonder that with such universal human needs, across all cultures, all genders, and all ages, the demand for technology, with the ***promises*** of "connecting people," has skyrocketed like nothing we have ever seen in history? Young adults have been particularly vulnerable to the changes in our "connecting" rituals. They have been socialized in the 21st century with the mass-marketed message, "Buy this device, because this is the *only* way people will get in touch with you and you will get laid."

Because we are so humanly hardwired for sexual connectivity in order for our species to survive, our subconscious minds say "Ok, I need *that* in order to get *this*." Let's be honest: the inspiration for Facebook was a group of young college guys who were using their knowledge of binary coding in order to check out girls. These hormonal, impatient, creative geniuses found a way, technically admirable at least, to improve the odds of the sexual chemistry experience.

With so much at stake and with the ultimate human reward awaiting, why wouldn't millions and millions of us jump blindly into this world of quick, easy, connection —

perhaps with less vulnerability and with a screen of protection in front of our ever-fragile hearts? Find love, intimacy, romance, and sex and friends and joy without ever having to actually "face" anyone? Excellent! What could possibly go wrong?

How is it that sometimes we can simply look at someone, someone that we've never met before, or sometimes someone that we have seen every day for years, and for some mysterious reason, when we least expect it, our brains start flooding with all sorts of "sex" chemicals that can feel like an electrical connection beyond our control? Along with the air that we breathe and the food that we eat, sex is right up there with the things that we crave and need.

This has been studied and philosophized about and analyzed for literally thousands of years. It is here, the connection between two humans on a level and intensity that has yet to be explained, that we have come to understand and accept that loving connections are the most powerful and most important part of the human experience.

Do we even have to question why inventors, engineers, scientists, and technophiles, understanding the insatiable demand for human connections, have worked tirelessly to create items and devices and "things" that might assist and help the population with this most important element?

We forgot one thing. This magical, mysterious, and most important part of our existence is *purely human*. What we now know is that it doesn't matter how fast your Internet speed is, how many people you list as a "friend," or how much you tweet, blog, post, and text. The fulfilling connections that we are all looking for must be accomplished through authentic human interactions that feed the soul in that most mysterious and magical way.

> "Oh my God, we're never going to be able to get married or have close relationships."
> —Ben, Emerson College

There is a growing number of young people who are honest enough to admit that the *"tap that," "bang a friend"* convenient sex apps that seem to be the cool thing to do actually are leaving them feeling cold, depressed, and soulless. When we ask the question, "How do you really feel about your digitally connected world?" the answer for many people is "We hate it."

Is this a call to throw away our technology? No, just the misconceptions. You can use technology only so far. You may have a fancy, fast car to get you to the party, but making the connections is **all you** once you show up. If you don't have the social skills because you've been too dependent on technology, your ability to make the connections you need will be compromised.

It is time for a reality check. We have spent the past 20 years having a love affair with technology, and what we have come up with is a society that is on the brink of insanity, more stressed out, more disconnected, lonely and isolated, depressed, and empty. In theory, the instant connectivity and 24/7 availability seemed like a good idea, but because we were blindsided by the allure of the gadgets, we simply forgot to appreciate and honor the beautifully flawed aspects of our humanity.

WATCH, LISTEN, LEARN

In the past decade I have worked closely with and have been surrounded by a generation of young adults whose thoughts on love, intimacy, sex, and romance dominate most of their brain space. And in the scope and timing of human development, they are right on target. During this digital period in our history, and with the introduction of new device after new device and the rise of social media and nonstop connectivity, the promises of ease and efficiency of emotionally fulfilling connections in the social realm never seemed to manifest. In fact, quite the contrary.

What I have found in the past six years is that our young population experiences more confusion, more stress, too many options, and dizzying expectations that lead to more anxiety and depression. I didn't need empirical research to support what I could clearly see happening. When we just look at people and really listen to them, we learn about them and we learn about ourselves. When we listen with the intention of learning, we get an understanding of how people are really feeling and what they're experiencing.

It's called emotional intelligence — a human skill set. It's a free app that comes with every person; it just needs to be used and cultivated. In July 2012, *Newsweek* magazine's cover story "iCrazy" dared to reveal a darker side of the technology explosion and its effects on our human apps.

In the beginning of the digital revolution, I did not start out as one of those "web skeptics" that the article refers to or as one of those who were considering the idea that "a new technology might influence how we think and *feel* — let alone contribute to a great American crack-up." Like most people, I was excited and fascinated with these new forms of communication that were viewed as "just another medium, a delivery system." However, as we began to incorporate these devices into our everyday lives, I could not ignore the changes to our social behavior.

From my daily observations of students who became clearly panicky with the request to "turn off phones" as class lectures were beginning, to the class-choreographed "checking for messages" ritual as soon as a break was announced, it was clear something was going on. A decade ago, students were squirming and checking the clock for the cigarette break. Now, the same behavior was happening, but instead of grabbing a pack of cigarettes, students grabbed their cell phones.

"Just another delivery system?" I couldn't help but disagree. Daily I listened to stories of confusion, with words like "addicted" and "compulsive" being casually tossed around. This book is the creation of some of those who were socialized in the middle of our 21st-century digital explosion and who are willing to share some insight and strategies that changed their perspective and values, as well as improving their personal relationships and love lives. It is in the spirit of sharing that we invite you to be a part of the solution.

Steve and Billi

Two months after my last semester ended, one of my students, Steve, tracked me down and stuck his head into my classroom as students were filing out and I was packing up my things. "Do you have a minute?" he asked. I hadn't seen him since he took the final exam during my last Interpersonal Communication course.

In that class, the main focus is on building our personal communication skills. We also learn about the effects of technology within our personal communication experiences, the nuts and bolts of how to communicate in order to fulfill those deep, more intimate, connections that we crave, and how to look at our digitally-heavy, overloaded world through the lens of a social scientist observing our human interactions.

Students are anxious to share their personal experiences as they look for strategies to improve their relationships. As part of the Interpersonal Communication class, students keep daily journals to record their findings and observations. We're together for 14 weeks, during which we work closely together, listening and learning from one another and offering emotional feedback when someone had a crazy miscommunication experience or Facebook disaster.

Because the class is pretty candid with sharing personal stories, we tend to get closer than most academic classes. "It was really important that Billi (short for Britney) and I let you know that, ah, we're together...ah, we kinda fell in love during your class." Steve's sincere smile was so heartwarming. "What!!!!" I couldn't help myself. "Oh my God...that is so wonderful...but, what about..." I knew that they had both been involved with other people during the course, as we had tried to resolve some of the communication issues they were having in their previous relationships. "So, what happened?"

"It was really interesting," Steve said. "My ex-girlfriend was so nonstop with the texting all day. I mean, she needed to know where I was, and what I was doing, and if I didn't text her back right away, then we got into a fight. So, we had been broken up for a while. [Steve revealed later that he originally took the class in order to figure out how to get better with keeping up with texting, Facebook, and other 21st-century connection devices.] Billi was going through some of the same stuff with her boyfriend, and so we were talking a lot as we were learning about all the stuff that goes on with real personal communication, the importance of autonomy, and now that we both learned how to, we just got closer and closer."

Steve and I continued to talk about how having a better understanding of the communication process and other elements of the human condition can be so powerful. As I told him how I'd love to use this story in the book and have him speak about it, he said, "I really support your work and what you're doing, but I need to confess something that I meant to tell you throughout the semester." "Uh-oh" I thought. Steve was looking down as he started. "When I was in my senior year [of high school] and with my ex-girlfriend, I stupidly sent her a 'sexting' message."

"Joni, you cannot imagine how things totally went out of control so fast. If we both hadn't been 18, I could be in jail." Now, you have to know that this is the sweetest, most compassionate kid you could ever meet. He continued, "I lost my scholarship money, humiliated myself and my family...it was just horrible. So, I wanted to let you know this up front in case you don't want me involved in your project." "Oh my God, Steve," I said. "Really, who better? There are so many kids who are finding themselves in so much trouble because of the technological power-pull and impulsivity; it's really important that there is more awareness."

"This was just such a horrible time in my life and for my family. There were so many times during class that I wanted to say something about this, especially when you were talking about the difference between mindful and mindless communication. I was totally not thinking, and it just happened so fast." He explained that before he even got home from school, his mother already knew about the incident. He had to go to court, and it was a total heart-wrenching experience. "I'm telling you this now, because if there is anything I can do to help other kids avoid this, I'm really up for it."

Sometimes we jump to condemn human mistakes instead of trying to understand each other. Perfectly healthy teens and young adults, who are just trying to figure out what's happening to themselves and their biological development and anthropologically conditioned DNA to keep the species going, can collide in a 21st-century world of digital connecting that moves at warp speed. Digital devices can compromise our logic.

> *According to 2012 statistics from the National Campaign to Prevent Teen and Unplanned Pregnancy, 71% of teen girls and 67% of teen guys who have sent or posted sexually suggestive content say they have sent/posted this content to a boyfriend or girlfriend. 48% of teens 13–19 and 62% of young adults 20–26 received a text of sexually explicit material. 36% of young adult women have posted nude or semi-nude photos of themselves.*

It's also important to understand that the brains of adolescents are just not biologically developed to comprehend consequences. It's one of the many reasons why restrictions are a normal part of a child's life. We've imposed restrictions on alcohol and driving after years of deadly consequences; it will be a shame if we can't learn from history before acting on this logical and common-sense principle when it comes to technology-influenced consequences.

THE GOAL

"Purpose, it's that little thing that lights a fire
under your ass…"
— R. Lopez/J.Marx, from *Avenue Q*

I want to be very clear that this is not an anti-technology book. This is about balance. I don't want you to start twitching with a nervous tic thinking I'm issuing a call to abolish cell phones or social media. The merits of today's communication technologies are nothing short of genius. The purpose of this book is to evaluate **how** we can use technology in the spirit of serving our humanity, rather than us serving the technology.

Every new device comes with a manual describing how to use it, but **not *how to use it within our society*.** During the past decade we have totally shifted the way we "connect" interpersonally, and as technology changes so rapidly, we have never quite had the time to establish a protocol for how to incorporate the new technology into our world with a thoughtful evaluation of the complexities and nuances of the communication process. In fact, we have been winging it — learning through trial and error. As much as we love the speed, convenience, and seeming efficiency of our 21st-century communication tools, we might be losing sight of authentic connectivity, intimacy, social skills, autonomy, and civility with one another, as we are developing greater dependence on devices instead of each other.

The purpose of this book is to evaluate how we are using technology, and to reaffirm our human values in order to become more discerning media consumers. We are exposed to millions of messages intended to persuade us to purchase every new piece of technology, with the underlying mediated message that "you **need** this to connect." The messages go to our innate fear of being "disconnected."

This book offers a little bit of insight into the bigger picture, showing what we might be sacrificing of ourselves and our personal development and the traditionally valued social skills of the next generation, because those things are not revenue-generating.

I understand the scope of the information technology industry and how this book may be received. However, I cannot continue to stand by and accept the ubiquitous "just the way it is today" attitude. We make social changes all the time in our society when things aren't working out the way we had planned, so why shouldn't we do the same thing in the digital world?

This is not intended to be a war against the gazillion dollar "connection industry"—it is a call for honesty. However, my emotions do run strong in the area of social justice. These are billion-dollar companies whose bottom-line profit remains the priority over implementing policy changes, particularly when it comes to the death and personal damage of a human being. I find the "collateral damage" philosophy of social media sites that ignore these issues to be pretty cold.

When the power executives in Silicon Valley are sending their kids to schools *without* any technology because they believe it's important for children to develop their social skills authentically, then why isn't that sentiment reinforced throughout our society? In the article "The Touch Screen Generation" for *The Atlantic* magazine, we find that the people who develop "educational apps" for kids impose strict guidelines and limit use of these devices for their own kids, admitting that "It can be too addictive, too stimulating for the brain." Where's the honesty? Where are the warnings to the general public? When will those same "thirty minutes, weekends only" restrictions become part of the general public's understanding of technology use for kids?

Perhaps there were some things that we overlooked. Maybe we just got all caught up in the whirlwind of the fast pace of new, cool inventions. Or what if, as some futurists are proposing, we mere mortals are simply not going to exist without the enhancement of digital devices?

For right now, my sincere purpose is to address some communication issues that are not working for us, offer some suggestions, and to do a little tweaking of our daily behavior in order to gain a greater sense of well-being and balance within our 24/7 digitally connected world.

PERSONAL DISCLOSURE

There are scientists and technophiles and also idealists and romantics. There are extroverts who gain energy from the people they surround themselves with, and introverts who beautifully observe the world around them with contemplative reflection. There are poets and musicians and chemists and biologists and laborers who set the foundation of the world we live in with their own creative and productive focus. The world needs variety. Variety gives us balance and makes great contributions to our society.

As we are officially in the "Information Age" right now, it seems the pendulum is in full swing into the quite incredible world of technology. When or *if* it ever moves back or even slows down a bit remains to be seen.

Full disclosure: this book is written through the lens of an idealist and romantic who believes in the power of the human spirit, authentic intelligence over artificial intelligence, genuine connections, vulnerability for intimacy, appreciation of autonomy, the transformative power of listening to understand and validate one another, using language impeccably, and "connecting" on a deeper level in order to meet and enrich our intrinsic needs and to restore respect and civility in our daily interactions with one another. I absolutely believe that if we could ever embrace a priority of simply trying to understand one another, we could begin to experience a personal and global evolution.

The communication process is as complex as the emotion-based human being. It cannot be reduced to the idea that communication is about the exchange of information or that technology can *do* the connecting for you. We are blessed to live in a world where the greatest minds, with their creativity and understanding of binary code, offer us a world of incredible tools and communication resources that can change the world in positive ways.

However, we have to remember that these devices are *only tools,* and that **you** are still the communicator. You are a human— mind, body and soul, and your humanness, with all your limitations, flaws, emotions and complexities, is perfection. There is not a thing in this world that can top the creation of the human, of you. You are human and you have all the apps you need. You are perfectly complete.

HOW TO USE THIS BOOK

I have to be honest with you. Whenever I mentioned that I was writing a book for this particular age group, I was usually met with some form of skepticism along the lines of "Does anyone even read books anymore?" Based on conversations with the teenagers and young adults in my life, in class discussions in my college courses, and in the spirit of listening to you, I thought I'd present this information in a way that you might best take it in.

According to current research, reading nonfiction and information-based books can be more challenging because of how we have been processing information over the past 20 years since living with the Internet. We'll get into that more in the chapter devoted to how our digital world has changed our brains. Apparently, unless we're reading a fabulous novel about suburbanites who are into handcuffs and bondage, sexually driven vampires, or superheroes, our attention span for taking in information has been compromised.

I have been told that young people "need" to line up laptop tabs in order to "fly between" Facebook, Twitter, and Instagram and that they need to constantly check phones for texts. The nonstop digital distractions happening while students do homework or read are today considered "normal." Research shows that our brains are being physically rewired to demand more stimulation within the learning process. So, you'll find that I have incorporated some "visual reinforcements" within the traditional reading experience.

The objective is for you to have the traditional experience of holding and reading a paper book. You can throw the book in a backpack or bag. There are places for you to jot down thoughts, scribble, reflect, and journal in your own handwriting, giving you a personal relationship with the book. However, if at times you'd like a visual reinforcement, the digital breaks reflect the material in the book. Log onto **CellingYourSoul.com,** open the "digital break" page, and click on the corresponding numbered icon.

As an educator, I can appreciate that we all have different learning styles. Some of us are visual learners; some are auditory. I believe technology can be very effective in *some* areas, so I'm just offering an option. However, as you are easing back into practicing and exercising your linear thinking brains, just the way you would increase your weights to build those muscles, try just reading and even just skimming and then taking a minute to think and reflect. The point is not to just *share* information. The point is for you to *process* information and turn it into knowledge. A major misconception of the 21st century is that we're supposed to "have" all this information. Total overkill. You are not a collector of data; you are a *thinker.*

In addition to the combination of reading and technology, the book provides some suggestions and strategies to improve your interpersonal communication skills. Researchers at the University of Arizona found that college students who spend more time engaging in conversations on a deeper level, for example, about politics, religion, or current events, are actually happier. These conversations support part of the human need for more meaningful and fulfilling social connections. I have included some conversation starters that can be useful throughout your day, and it could be *really* interesting if you could convince a couple of friends to join you and read this book as a group. You are encouraged to discuss, debate, and challenge some of the topics.

So, let's start with just turning off your phone. Here's the first thing to challenge yourself with: can you actually "turn off" your phone for a period of time? Not silence, but actually "off." Some of you might say "no big deal," but others might be feeling a bit uncomfortable. Either way, it's one way of learning about yourself and your relationship with your technology.

Business communication 101: never bring up a problem without offering some solutions. Or, to borrow the slogan from a Zendik bumper sticker I saw, "Stop your bitchin' and start a revolution."

Try This

Take this book to read at a park, a coffee shop, bar, restaurant...don't have your phone on the table in front of you. Have your phone actually turned off and put away if you can. If someone crosses your path, look up and nod or smile, that is, if they actually look up from *their* digital devices enough to make eye contact. You will stand out just by the simple concept that it is rare to see a young person reading an actual book *au naturel*, meaning without wires coming out of your ears. See if you end up exchanging any cordial small talk. As I said, I am a romantic at heart, so maybe you will meet the love of your life...please let me know!

The goal is to have you think...yes, think critically, deeply, and discuss at length, *in person* with one another, with cell phones put away...just for a little while. Think and talk and have a conversation without any distractions. Observe your friend's faces when they get all hyper or are deep in thought. Goof on them, challenge them, and laugh with them.

Perhaps we can move toward a national understanding of our human communication needs and create some healthy boundaries. Imagine someday being able to live "off line" for a while to get your head together? And... actually, have it be OK! Or, being able to go on vacation for two weeks and feel that your job will be there and the world will continue to spin on its axis if you take some time to recharge?

The bottom line is that this is *your* world and your future. You can shape it any way you want. Social norms are fluid, and when they are challenged, they change over and over again.

Chapter 2

w t f

"When we start communicating with our thumbs
we're in big trouble."
— Media Literacy Student, 2006

"Seriously, what the fuck!" We were just getting
ready to start a Media Literacy class when I heard a student
say that as he was slamming his Verizon flip phone down on
the desk. I could see he was really frustrated. I asked him
what was going on, and he said, "It's my girlfriend with the
f'n texts. She's nonstop. I'm just about to answer her, and it
takes me so much longer, that right when I'm trying to answer her, she's shootin' off another one asking me what's going on...I can't have a f'n minute to even think...I hate it!"
Back then, texting on a flip phone required a whole new set
of skills.

It seemed like every other guy in the class said something to the effect of "Right...me too, dude!" Most of the fe-
males in the class seemed to be smirking a bit, with the
occasional side comment along the lines of "Why does it take
guys so long to answer?" The pissed-off student looked up to
me with a precautionary warning look and said, "Seriously,
when we start communicating with our thumbs, we're in big
trouble," nodding his head a bit as if to say, "You'll see." I
think he was right.

Up until about 2006, the cell phone was used by most
adults as a form of security or in case of an emergency, was
usually stored in a briefcase, purse, or backpack, and was

occasionally checked for messages. Many of my students think back fondly of their days in high school, when having a beeper was either way cool if what you got was a message from a friend, or a major technological inconvenience when you had to call your mother. The ol' pager, for those who had them for work, was fantastic for employers who now knew that they had their workers "on call" for emergency shift-work, but not so great for employees who might have been able to avoid going in to work because "Ah shucks, I wasn't home to get the call." So, the excuses were gone.

We were moving into the "on-call" era. Years ago, doctors used to report that they knew they couldn't really unwind. Their periods of being "on call" kept their bodies and minds in a certain type of heightened anticipatory level of awareness... just waiting for the little "beep." Now it's only a few years later, and we have become the Pavlovian nation. We have been so conditioned to react to every beep, buzz, vibration, or ringtone that we are constantly on call, 24 hours a day, 7 days a week. For most Americans, kids to adults, there is zero downtime. We are always on.

A friend of mine and I were talking about the fact that only a few years ago, if you were working all day and using your office computer, before you left for the evening you would simply turn off your computer, say goodbye to work, and actually be OK with the fact that any email that came in after you left would just have to wait until the next morning. Can you imagine? And...that was a pretty acceptable expectation. If someone sent out a work email after 6:00 P.M., the sender assumed they wouldn't hear back until the next day...and...that was actually OK. The work/home life boundary was clear.

To even be talking about email as an antiquated form of communication in 2012–2013 seems crazy, but it really goes to show the exponential surge in technology. The problem is that when each new digital device appears, we start to work it into our world without trying to figure out *how* it should be incorporated into our lives.

For thousands of years we used ink on paper to communicate and express our thoughts. Then, at the turn of the 20th century, we developed broadcasting to the masses and used telephones to talk to each other interpersonally when we were not physically together. We had a clear understanding of phone etiquette, and we taught our children how to answer the phone while showing respect to the person calling. As children, we were forced to learn how to talk to adults, petrified that we might get someone's parent on the other end of the line. We knew the drill. We knew exactly how to deal with it, because we grew up with the same modeled behavior that was reinforced by grandparents and parents. If you wanted to "connect," you *had* to call.

Even at the turn of the 21st century, our interpersonal communication values remained traditional. It was only a few years ago that people were outraged and put legislation into place restricting telemarketing calls to homes, because the constant phone ringing was considered intrusive, especially if calls came during the highly valued dinner hours. Remember how we valued the sanctity of an uninterrupted evening? In one very short decade, however, we have totally changed the way we communicate with one another. Today, it's not uncommon for families across the country, or friends gathering for an evening, to all walk in holding their phones in front of them, like the holy grail, and place them down in clear view. Some even need to keep their personal technology closer so they can "feel" it physically on their bodies. We're all just waiting...waiting for the sign or sound that says, "Someone wants you."

Many of us are familiar with the concept of "conditioning" from Ivan Pavlov's Nobel prize-winning research in the early 1900s. Pavlov's dogs started to salivate with the ringing bell that said "reward/food = happy." If we apply that logic to our ringing cell phones, we should be the happiest people ever, right? However, research shows that we are not as happy as we thought we might be. In just this past decade, we have become a nation living on heightened alertness, with a confusing and ever-changing protocol of work and personal communication.

We're constantly dealing with unrealistic expectations, whether we're the ones trying to "connect" with someone or being the ones expected to respond, losing a little part of our humanity with one another because our instant-gratification communication process has eroded all our patience with people. It just seems to be a bit much. We've come a long way in a short time.

IT *WAS* COOL

I was thrilled to be at the forefront of cell phone usage. In the 80s and 90s, before cell phones became the social norm they are today, I was an entertainment reporter. I was lucky to be using a ginormous phone that nestled safely in what looked like a titanium briefcase – like something out of a James Bond movie. I even had to put a metal antenna on my car roof for the phone to work. I felt like the coolest person in the world! The phone weighed a ton, airport security people were curious and amazed, and even rock stars were flippin' out when I interviewed them live backstage using the phone instead of a microphone. It was pretty convenient to just use the phone instead of cumbersome remote setups.

The briefcase phone turned into a bag phone, which was still cumbersome and was often left in the car. Over the past 20 years, the phones kept on getting smaller and smaller. The more portable they got, the more affordable and prevalent they became. Since up until 2004 or 2005 only adults could afford them, we all understood that using the phone in a social setting was limited to "something important." We still carried over our indoctrinated social skills and phone manners from our childhoods. Does anyone remember excusing yourself to make a phone call and then apologizing for the interruption when you returned?

It was very clearly understood, *way* back about six or seven years ago, that if you answered your phone and carried on a conversation in the presence of other people, you were being rude. Period. Most people today will *not* necessarily disagree with that. Putting it out for a vote with my students, I usually get unanimous head-nodding and laughing as we compare stories of said "asshole" experiences. Yet, when I ask, "Do you ever do it?" I get the same response. "Yup"... lots of laughing, and admitting, "Oh, I can be a total asshole." Many students start the ubiquitous defense with phrases like, "Oh, but, it was really important" or "I was waiting for that call," and always give an excellent reason why they had to be rude to the person in front of them.

There has been a profound change in our human interactions with one another, and we're not feeling good about it. Students have pulled me aside to ask, "Why do you think I have to have my Facebook tab open all the time?" People are distracted, walking across the streets with their faces focused on their phones, living in their own worlds instead of the world around them. We even resort to technology (apps like "Freedom," which blocks Internet connectivity) in order to get the digital break we need and cannot rely on our human self-control to get. Schools are even creating "Internet-Free zones" in order to help students focus on homework or other important tasks because they have acknowledged that the digital pull is too strong for some.

It seems like we're in the story of the Emperor's New Clothes. You remember: the Emperor was told that his new clothes were invisible to anyone who was either unfit for his job or hopelessly stupid. Not wanting to admit that he himself couldn't see his clothes, the naked Emperor proudly led the parade. People in the crowd looked to each other to see how they should react (social norms are developed by looking to others to see how to behave); they clapped and smiled and didn't dare mention the obvious.

It's not much different today. As we watch people personally connecting to their own devices, tuning out the world around them, we've adopted an attitude of "If you can't beat 'em, join 'em."

Some wonderful documentaries have exposed the problems and offered the latest scientific studies on the effects of our cell phone use. "Growing Up On Line," "Digital Nation," "The Facebook Obsession," and "Crackberry'd" all demonstrate the problem, citing supporting studies and using impressive experts. However, all seem to end with a shoulder shrug, caving in to the idea that this is just the world we live in. The information and research from these documentaries hasn't captured mainstream attention. However, would it even matter? We're so in love with our devices that we don't want to know about the negative ramifications. What happened to us? Are cell phones really that addicting?

On March 14, 2012, Jon Stewart ran a piece on homeless people being used as "hot spots" for cell reception. As Stewart explained, homeless people were wearing T-shirts that said "I Am a Hot Spot." Stewart was flabbergasted with the fact that the T-shirts said nothing about the fact this was actually a person. "Rather than train homeless people to become computer workers, they (the advertisers at SXSW) train them to *become* [computer] *equipment!*" he explained. It seems we've lost all respect for humanity.

How is this a technological *advancement* to better the society that we're living in? Do we need to rethink the word human*kind*? I think we can do better.

In 2007, after countless classroom discussions on the impact of social media and cell phones within our mediated world, and after seeing a T-shirt on a student that read "Don't talk to me if you're not a computer screen," I was asked to develop an Interpersonal Communication class. Because of my education in psychology, my communication classes include an emphasis on the psychological complexities of the human communication process. During these classes, I really started to understand how students and teens were struggling with the daily issues of trying to figure out how the hell to communicate on a personal level within our digital world with its endless options. How do we know when to send an email instead of making a phone call? How do you respond to a text when you might not have the ability to text back?

At that point, there were no rules, suggestions, or expert advice, because we were all learning as-we-go as the technology was rapidly unfolding. Even when someone did come up with suggestions, for example the book *Send* about email etiquette, the information was almost outdated by the time the book was published. We were now moving on to texting and social media. We were all using the trial-and-error approach. Some of the "errors" had irrevocable consequences.

> *In 2009, research showed that eight percent of companies had fired someone for social media behavior.*

In Massachusetts, a teacher was fired for calling the parents of her students "snobby" in a Facebook posting. The irony was that she actually taught the computer technology class and believed that she was only "speaking" privately to her "friends." In Georgia, another teacher was forced to resign because she posted a picture of herself, at the Guinness factory while on vacation in Ireland, drinking a beer.

The stories are endless: people calling their bosses stupid and their jobs boring, or posting insensitive jokes. "Does anyone know where I can find a very discreet hitman?" was posted by a professor at a Pennsylvania college right after the shooting at the University of Alabama in February 2010. What used to be considered simple slips of the tongue were now carrying stronger implications. Comments and photos were becoming an indelible part of the Internet environment and of the lives of individuals who posted them. This is an issue that continues to cause problems, even now that we intellectually understand the ramifications. What we haven't seemed to learn, however, is that the communication process is influenced by emotions.

The objective of communicating with another person is to share a thought, make a connection, have your feelings validated, be understood, reach out for some form of a "Yeah, I hear you." Yet with all the different communication options to choose from, the mindless nature of communications in front of a computer screen often leads to the one thoughtless moment that can ruin a life.

Many teens and young adults seem puzzled and curious as to why their communication isn't working. Although they have the latest and greatest gadgets and hundreds of "friends," they aren't feeling good. I watched as many class discussions turned into Facebook or Tumbl'r therapy because of an impulsive "post." Students walked in saying, "I couldn't wait to bring this [story] up in class."

"I was having a bad day, so I went on Facebook to tell my friends and I was really upset because nobody 'liked' it. That made me feel worse."
— Media Literacy Student, 2010

Our relationship with our cell phones and smartphones and digital connections to the world is overwhelmingly powerful. It has become a huge part of our society and has a strong impact on many people. We know that in life there are always positive and negatives to everything. It seems naïve and irresponsible of us not to make room for some real discussions and exposure of the dark side of our 21st-century communication behaviors.

This is the Information Age. We can find out everything about anything with one click. However, it is important to understand that information is not necessarily knowledge. Turning information into knowledge requires thought, and then synthesizing those thoughts with our own values, personalities, and vast intellectual and emotional data. We're humans. We're complex. To market and sell the idea that human interaction, communicating, and "connecting" to one another is a mere "information in/information out" formula is not only an over-simplification but is insulting and damaging, especially for young developing minds. We're told that if we're on Facebook or have the latest smartphone with 4G technology, we will be "connecting."

However, as humans we crave emotional connections. The connections we need to thrive are on a deeper, more personal level. You don't get that by being an *audience* to "friends'" posts, tweets, and blogs. Yet, when we post or text a thought, we feel like we're being an efficient and productive communicator, being able to "share" with so many people at once. To the receiver, our posts sometimes feel cold, impersonal, insensitive, or rude.

Our younger generation is being socialized with the misconception that communication is about exchanging information, news, and personal updates on our day-to-day life experiences. Interpersonal communication is about bonding and sharing on an emotional level – not necessarily some deep emotion, but at a personal level. I'm sorry to tell you, but that actually takes a little effort in building social skills and emotional intelligence. Despite great technological advances, there is no app for that.

As new research is being published, and as my students have discovered during our work together, constant exposure to this lazy communication approach erodes our relationships, our development, and our very spirit. The messages we are sending at a subconscious level are that we value our technology and our devices more than the child or person right in front of us.

My initial thought in developing an interpersonal communication class in the digital age was that we need to understand that we are in a different world, and that there is a great generational divide today just as was first seen in the 50s with rock and roll and in every decade since then. I figured that we're going to have to adjust to the fact that this generation is communicating differently than the generations before. We're going to have to figure out how to incorporate their age-appropriate communication within a multigenerational communication community. Or, in the terms used by many researchers, we need to integrate digital natives with the digital immigrants. What I didn't expect to learn is that the natives are restless. And, they are looking for an escape.

In the past six years I have listened to more than 1,000 college-age students discussing the issues of communicating in the 21st century. This is the generation who have been most affected by the sudden shift. As much time as they spend using technology, it seems they can spend as much time complaining about the effects it's having in their lives: stress, lack of mental energy, demanding expectations, lack of privacy, lack of down time, increased distraction, public humiliation, erosion of self-esteem, identity issues, anxiety, moments of feeling violated through social media, confusion, fear of being out of the loop or missing out, wondering whether to stay on or get off Facebook and why they feel the need to have their Facebook, Twitter, and Instagram tabs up all the time, and an ***increase*** in loneliness. As illogical as that sounds in the world of over-connectedness, there is a growing feeling of being disconnected.

When it comes to matters of the human experience, where love, understanding, validation, security, mental health, and happiness are the objectives, we are all pretty much the same. The human communication process is all about getting our very personal needs met; there is no generation gap. We are *all* human to the core.

IT'S SO SAD

Each semester, my students are asked to observe personal communication interactions among commuters on public transit, family members, roommates, or friends or in their own relationships, and to analyze the effectiveness of the interpersonal communication process through the lens of a social scientist.

Students keep a running journal and come to class to discuss their experiences and submit the journal for review. Most students report this to be an eye-opening experience. "Oh my God, it was so sad," one student reported. "This whole family was out to dinner and everyone was doing their own thing...the kids on their phones [texting], parents either talking to someone else or texting. The "It's so sad" comment has been a popular running theme in many of the students' journal entries.

Those comments usually involve kids and parents, or their own brothers and sisters. Students find it "so sad that my brother thinks Facebook is the place to journal all his own private issues" or "so sad that the only time my sister talks to the family is when she's punished and her phone is taken away from her." One particular comment that sparked an interesting class discussion was, "So sad to see a woman at the beauty parlor who was getting her hair done and just kept giving her little baby her iPad to play with. I mean the woman was there for like two hours and all this little kid did was play with a computer." "Well," I said, "how different is that from handing a baby some keys to jingle or a book or their binky, as long as it keeps them quiet and, well, pacified?" The responses from some were "Well, I guess it isn't any different," but from quite a few I received different forms of "It's just not right." However, the students couldn't really figure out why it didn't *feel* right to them.

Perhaps it's because things like pacifiers have an expiration date on them. Developmentally, they are used during early childhood as babies are learning to cope and self-soothe. At the appropriate time, babies are weaned off pacifiers so that their human apps can develop. They learn to cope and handle their anxiety without needing an outside form of security, such as a pacifier. So, what happens when we are conditioned at birth to look to the cell phone, iPad, or other form of technology to distract us when we feel anxious or to make us feel secure, and when there is no social pressure, ever, to wean off it?

Are we cultivating too much dependence? In February 2012, a report on the evening news talked about the updated research on "nomophobia." "No-Mo-What?" I thought. Nomophobia, first coined in 2008 in the UK, is the name of the disorder associated with the fear of being without your cell phone. The word literally translates to "no mobile phobia." Yup...it has a name. According to *The Telegraph*, British researchers have been studying this phenomenon for years. The 2012 survey of 1,000 people revealed that 66% of the population suffers from a sense of panic and anxiety if they are away from their cell phones. There have been other global studies regarding this behavior. One study of medical students in India reports their data as "indicative of nomophobia to be an emerging problem of the modern era." These studies coincide with the observations and discussions I have been having in the classroom during the same period.

One little experiment we've done in the classroom involves checking to see how everyone feels when I have students exchange phones with one another. Students say "It just feels weird," or "It's like it's too personal, like holding someone's underwear," or "I don't like holding someone else's phone and I really don't like seeing [him] holding my phone. I just want to say, just give it back."

Then we escalate the experiment. How does it feel if you don't "see" someone holding your phone...what if it's in their backpack? Or, what if I collect them and hold them for you? Students have said they first worry that we'll forget or that I'll walk out without giving the phones back. So, their stress came from imagining that they might not have the phone later. After the initial worry, students said they relaxed a bit and could get back into the class work, but they all agreed that they experienced some degree of fear of being separated from their device.

We are now starting to see the results of peer-reviewed scientific studies on the addictive characteristics of technology. Historically, however, data about feelings and attitudes, considered subjective, can be easier to dismiss. According to David Giles, author of *Illusions of Immortality–A Psychology of Fame*, "If a psychological phenomenon can't be studied in the laboratory, yielding hard data that can be analyzed statistically, it has generally been neglected as a potential research topic."

Sometimes common sense prevails; sometimes you have to go with your gut. I remember my mother telling my sister and me that when we were babies, all the older aunts would yell at her for picking us up every time we cried. They would remind her that Dr. Spock, the eminent authority on babies at the time, would say "You're spoiling them." My mother would just say, "My baby is crying, so that means she needs something, so I am going to pick her up." Of course, now we have come to know the importance of attending to a baby's cry throughout the day. Crying is a pretty instinctual form of communicating to have needs met.

Talking about going with your gut and the power of common sense, there is a great scene in the movie *The King's Speech.* Actor Jeffrey Rush, who plays Lionel, the voice coach to Colin Firth's King George VI, is watching the King smoke a cigarette:

> Lionel: *"I believe sucking smoke into your lungs will kill you."*
>
> The King: *"My physicians say it relaxes the throat."*
>
> Lionel: *"They're idiots."*
>
> The King: *"They've all been knighted."*
>
> Lionel: *"Makes it official then."*

Today's technology and our digital devices are here to stay. Unless, as with cigarettes, people start dying from cell phone use (and so far, there is no significant research that undeniably connects physiological problems to destructive radio waves), cell phones will remain a growing part of our world. And consider the fact that when it comes to addictive behavior, even knowing that the consequences may be death doesn't necessarily make people change. The reward often outweighs the consequences. King George VI, after all, died of lung cancer.

What is the cost of our easy, convenient, and fast communication lifestyle? We thought McDonalds and Burger King drive-ins were a fantastic contribution to our world, and look what a steady diet of that type of over-consumption has done to us. We embraced them as a convenient substitute for the hassle of a home-cooked meal. It took us over 50 years to see the fast food surge as a contributory *part* of an obese and diabetic society. We are conditioned to believe that anything that's fast, easy, and convenient makes life better. If it's faster, it's better. And so we overdo everything, including our relationship with media.

After years of concrete studies on the physiological affect of fast food and, in addition, one impactful documentary, *Supersize Me*, the media attention and increased awareness of the problem led to a positive change: menu options creating greater balance and choice. However, when it comes to the social sciences, we cannot generate such impactful and impartial physiological and biological data. There are no blood tests for information overload or compulsive texting.

We need to become more comfortable with the paradox that some things can be **both** beneficial *and* destructive. We are not good with living in the grey area. We have this black and white, either-or, way of thinking in our culture, when the truth is that two apparent opposites can coexist. A great tool in the hands of someone who is not equipped, who is careless, or who does not have any foresight of potential consequences can be disastrous.

As we invite technological advances into our world, we must understand that they are intended to replace some things that have been long-established parts of our culture. Where there are gains, there are losses. It's important that we weigh the benefits over the sacrifices and proceed cautiously as the tradeoffs start unfolding. Unfortunately, as we all know in our instant-gratification culture, this kind of benefit/sacrifice analysis can be impossible to actually practice. Just because technology is well intended doesn't mean that it's correct or is without drawbacks.

"Just because we're doing something, doesn't make it right. I equate it with the automobile, like if we invented the automobile today, would we say, I know, we'll run it on a finite fossil fuel, we'll export a half a trillion dollars of our GDP, we'll spend hundreds of billions of dollars on our military to protect that interest and it will pollute the environment."
— Brad Pitt, *The Daily Show,* February 1, 2012

The point is, we can make adjustments. Social norms are supposed to change according to our needs.

There is enormous pushback against anyone who speaks out about the negative affects of technology. You're instantly branded with an anti-tech label. I have a smartphone and use GPS all the time. I also know that using GPS means I will probably never be able to get to the same place without it, as I never have to pay attention to landmarks or surroundings. I am simply driving like a robot that can respond to commands. Am I being lazy, or am I on total information overload because I have been bombarded with emails and texts and expectations to respond to so many people that the idea of having to think about one more thing, like directions to a restaurant, makes me want to implode?

I'm just looking for an honest dialogue about the influences of our digitally enhanced world of today. The people I talk to think the same way, yet we feel stuck. Is technology serving us in the most beneficial way, or are we serving technology? Are all these gadgets things we really *need,* or is the need *being created* in order to contribute to billions of dollars in device sales and subsequent advertising?

You simply cannot get into a conversation about contemporary communication etiquette without having it turn into some type of complaint session debating what is acceptable or rude, or without people saying they felt offended by others taking calls or texts in the middle of a conversation. Yet, you might not say anything because you are mentally "reserving the right" to be rude right back should *you* want to "tweet," "text," or take a call when it's your turn. We're seeing a negative impact on our civility and respect for one another, and that wears at our souls.

As Nicholas Carr writes in his best selling book *The Shallows: What the Internet Is Doing to Our Brains*, "We may be wary of what our devices are doing to us, but we're using them more than ever. And yet, history tells us, it's only against such powerful cultural currents that countercultural movements take shape." Carr explains at the end of his book that when he was first writing and researching, he often felt like he was "paddling a very small and empty rowboat." I can relate.

After years of intense discussions and hundreds of personal stories from student's essays, social science experiments, case studies, and personal time spent with a lot of young adults, it became clear to me that this generation knows they're in trouble and they're not quite sure what to do. Many have asked for professional "communication" feedback about some troubling situation rooted in miscommunication or hurt feelings. Many students have said that they're really "concerned about" younger brothers or sisters who are using the Internet and social media to "journal everything" about their lives, or who won't look up from their phones, or who feel uncomfortable when they are having face-to-face conversations.

This book is not intended to be a condemnation of technology or scientific advances. This book is really about exploring the human condition within 21st-century communication tools. The point is *not* to simplify what we're doing today as good or bad; it's to reexamine our human values and come up with and implement a simple protocol that puts people first. We need to know how important it is to connect to ourselves by disconnecting with the world, and how important it is to live an authentic life in the real world and not through the lives of others or through media. And, most importantly, we need to have that be not only accepted, but honored and embraced by society.

"I can text while I'm in 'downward dog' [yoga position]."
— Media Lit Student, 2010

During many class discussions and revealing and honest conversations about media and communication in the digital age, when I shared some basic communication principles, my students have said outright "You should do something about this," or things like "See, people don't know this." Or, in other words, "People of our generation, who were socialized in the past decade, don't have a frame of reference for communication with one another before the digital takeover."

Those of us who were born before 1985 forget just how differently this generation has been socialized. My generation just assumed that our kids would be fine in this new exciting digital era. Everyone seemed to be functioning, and we actually came to become dependent on young people's innate ability to navigate a world that was foreign to us. They became our sources for technological instruction, or even the ones responsible for doing all the technological things we didn't "have a mind for." We didn't plan on this, but it happened. This generation took on the role of family "techie" whether they wanted it or not.

When we're not really paying attention, sometimes we can drift away. We didn't pay attention to what has been happening to the social and communication skills of an entire generation, and they have found themselves in the middle of a sea of digital devices. What I have learned is that when they do a little back-pedaling, making up for and learning about the fundamentals of the communication process, and then really practice communicating in more authentic connections, many students report important and productive changes in their lives and relationships.

Building authentic communication skills remains a major priority in the grand scope of our lives. We now know that we cannot allow digital devices to bypass the rather difficult, very human, and never-ending task of learning how to communicate with one another in a way that allows our personal and professional needs to be met. I have seen students go from depressed and confused to happier and more self-confident with very small changes. It is a thrill to hear from students whose relationships with their parents and family members have improved, whose love lives have changed, and who have gotten jobs. (One particular student was hired specifically for his "good communication skills" by, ironically, Apple).

So, here's to opening up a real conversation, with thinking critically, analyzing, weighing the pros and cons, understanding the long-term ramifications of this trajectory, and making adjustments.

By the way, in the story of the Emperor, one little boy had the courage to speak out against the nervous crowd and say, "Hey, the Emperor doesn't have any clothes on!" Sometimes one little voice — a writer in a rowboat, a teacher with compassion, or a pissed-off student — can have an impact on the powerful empire.

Chapter 3

No App for Life

"How Come Everything I Think I Need,
Always Comes with Batteries?"
— John Mayer

While watching television, with its never-ending commercials for the latest in 4G technology, I heard one ad refer to a device as having "more than 500,000 apps." This ad made me think, or actually do my best imitation, of Amy Poehler at the SNL news desk. "Really...really...we need 500,000 apps these days, really?" I'm sure that right now there are a lot of brilliant, creative people heading into work psyched to spend hours coding a new app that we won't even know we need until they have created it.

However, it seems that what we really need is a greater appreciation of our own *human* apps. Honestly, we're pretty amazing as is, and I'm starting to get insulted by the mediated message that seems to promote the idea that we are less than perfectly complete unless we have the latest and greatest, smallest, fastest device to supplement the inadequacies of our limited humanness.

Isn't the purpose of inventions to create things that enhance and enrich the human experience? The phone was invented to bring us together, which it does, but are we at the point of overkill? Actually, according to a Kaiser Family Foundation Study on media use, we spend more time listening to music, playing games, and watching TV on cell phones than we spend talking on them. When the media was buzzing with the release of the new iPad, the members of the band Green Day were being interviewed. Reporters backstage asked "So, what do you think of the new iPad?" Billy Jo Armstrong said that in this "constant barrage of technology...it blows my mind...I'm not quite sure when is enough, enough?"

3

If smartphones, which are personal robots with all the answers, can think for us, speak for us, tell us where to go and how to get there, and remind us what to do and where we have to be, are we in some ways devaluing our human relations and dependence on one another? Remember when we used to ask our parents or friends for answers or assistance?

It isn't always about just getting information. It's about having a human interaction that meets our human needs. It's not always about getting the facts; rather it's about knowing whether someone else knew that fact. Here's a sad loss. Remember what it was like when we were trying to think of who starred in what movie, or which band sang a certain song, or what movie won the Oscar last year? You always had that "go to" person.

I grew up in a show business and musical family and always knew my mother had the answer to everything. She wasn't always thrilled with the challenge or with the pressure from our expectations that she would know the answer or be able to name that tune in the first three notes. However, her track record was extraordinary, and we could feel the sense of accomplishment she felt when she'd get it right, without a moment of hesitation. The tone of her voice on the other end of the phone allowed us to actually hear the sweet sound of victory as she simply said, with a triumphant grin, "Anything else?"

I was the queen of useless knowledge for anything in the pop culture world of the 80s and 90s, proudly boasting that *that* was my era. However, I don't get many calls from my friends with the "Joni will know this" challenge anymore. Who needs us trivia queens when we have Google? Our contemporary communication devices can make worldly connections; however, they eliminate some of the more important emotional and human connections that support our personal identity and our intimate relationships.

Technophiles keep inventing things that replace the jobs of humans, including the role that each of us has in our circle of friends and family. Malcolm Gladwell writes about the concept of "transactive memory" based on the work of University of Virginia psychologist David Wegner. Because the human brain can only handle so much, we have developed the strategy of storing stuff that we need to remember with our partners, family members, and friends. According to his research, "When people know each other well, they create an implicit joint memory system, a transactive memory system, which is based on an understanding about who is best suited to remember what kinds of things." In other words, people need people. These are the relationships that feed the soul. As Gladwell reflects, "transactive memory is part of what intimacy means."

Intimacy and the ability to trust those closest to you are what strengthen our personal development. Like my family with the show business trivia, every family can identify the transactive memory system that is unique to each individual in the family unit. Everyone has their unique talents, so we end up designating that particular person to be, for example, the "grand holder of all that is food related" or the one who "names all the relatives at family gatherings." I am happy that my best friend can remember dates and years, and even what we were wearing on a school trip in the fifth grade. Because she can, I don't even have to try.

These bonded relationships are unique to our human experience and our needs to be valued. Relationships should be cherished rather than discounted because technology is being sold as an improvement of our human limitations. Understanding your role in the transactive memory system of your circle is important to your own self-identity, and if you can fulfill your duty when called upon, you feel a great sense of satisfaction. When you're the "go to" person, and you "got it," well, that's very cool and feels good. So much more satisfying than Google.

Try This
Think about your own "memory keepers." Who's in charge of what memories?   What is *your* memory role?   Write, scribble, doodle....

_____

_____

_____

_____

_____

WALL E WORLD

We are immersed in a world that is being described as the "robotic moment." MIT technology and society professor Sherry Turkle has been researching the human relationships within the growing field of robotic advances, and offers an in-depth view of where we might be headed in her latest book *Alone Together – Why We Expect More from Technology and Less from Each Other.* Her solid research supports and corroborates the feelings, discussions, and stories that I have had in my classroom and around friends and family, which leads me to believe that millions of people all over are having the same feelings and concerns.

Turkle interviewed hundreds of children who were brought up with robotic toys (remember Furbies?) and observed how they related emotionally to toys with human traits. Turkle has worked with young kids, high school and college students, parents, those in the corporate world, and even with the elderly, who are given robotic pets to keep them company in their old age. Her research demonstrates that we do develop emotional connections with inanimate objects, whether toys for a child, computers, or mobile devices.

As we are now entering the 24/7 personal assistant software age, with the robotic Siri, are we entering a slippery slope? If this is the path we're going to head down, isn't it important to ask whether Siri and her equivalents are going to enrich and enhance humanity? If we keep inventing things so that we humans don't have to answer each other's questions, depend on one another, or look to each other for answers, then shouldn't we be asking the question, "What are *we* here for?" What is our purpose if we keep inventing things that replace human functions?

IBM spokesman and vice president of innovation Bernie Meyerson issued a digital press release full of excitement about the technology that is going to be invented in the next five years. There will be some amazing innovations in renewable energy, eyeball-reading technology so that we won't need passwords anymore, and mind-reading technology. Here's this guy all happy and excited about this technology that will read our minds and pull our thoughts, and he said, "So, we won't have any need for literacy."

He had an "isn't that great" tone in his voice and a big smile. I had to watch it again to be sure I had it right. So, we are going to create these new people for the planet, and then what? No reading or writing? To be fair, other reports suggested that this technology would be for the benefit of paraplegics so they could live more independently. That would be an excellent service. However, we have seen technology spiral into areas where it wasn't invited.

Are we conditioning the next generation to value technology *rather* than people? The question to ask with regard to all new forms of technology and innovation is *"**Just because we can, does it mean we should?**"* The reality is that we are socialized to exist in a world of instant gratification and black-or-white thinking. However, we have to start using our own human apps to wrap our heads around the fact that these issues are complex; they require critical thinking and deep contemplation on ethics and morality. In other words, we cannot just Google the answer to some of the issues that are affecting our society and our future.

As technology enters many areas of our lives, and at such a pace that we don't have any time to think things through, we must constantly ask ourselves about our purpose. Are we just racing through to get to some finish line? What is the purpose of the collective moments that make up our lives?

One particular story in Turkle's book that disturbed me was the story about a man who is struggling with visiting his mother in a nursing home. He wants to spend more time with her, but of course his life is busy. The mother was one of the people used in Turkle's studies on robotic companionship. The elderly woman seemed to derive some good feelings from the human substitute. Turkle writes about the fact that the man "took comfort in how much his mother enjoyed talking to [the robot] Paro, and said it made 'walking out that door' so much easier when he visited her at the nursing home."

Turkle weighs the pros and cons, and there are many of both. For example, using a robot may put less of a burden on those caring for the elderly, yet there is also the question of dignity for the elderly. If you're under 25, this might not have the emotional impact for you right now compared to someone who is 70. However, the direction that our society is going in shows that you *will* be the ones who will be most affected by the decisions being made today.

In other words, you will be the one reliant on a Nursebot to wipe your future ass. Turkle ends her chapter with the announcement that the inventors of the Paro companions are opening new stores here in the U.S.

> "I've got gadgets and gizmos a plenty...but who cares...I want more...I want to be where the people are..."
> — Ariel, *The Little Mermaid*

Who decides what is brought into our world and what becomes obsolete in our everyday lives? In his book *Democracy and Technology*, author Richard Sclove explains how the Amish first "ask themselves how a particular set of technologies would affect their community." They make their decisions based on a solid vision of their values.

For us to adopt this model, we'd have to have strong convictions in our social values, which unfortunately seem to vacillate with every new piece of technology that we're offered. Wouldn't this be a case of us serving technology, rather than technology serving humanity? Sclove says that "the problem of achieving consensual answers is of much less concern than our failure even to begin debating crucial questions, in this case, technology's political and cultural dimensions."

Here's a perfect example. Cursive writing has been a fundamental staple of our communication culture for thousands of years. In fact, the Declaration of Independence and other historical documents are written in cursive. However, because of the demands of standardized testing, many schools in the public education system were allowed to "opt out" of teaching the Palmer method.

So, on a practical level, we are going to have a big communication gap if someone who is 20 and unable to read cursive is in the workforce with someone who is 40 and only writes in cursive. I don't remember voting on a decision to abolish a universal form of communication so that my future grandchildren will never be able to read the Gettysburg Address or recognize the names of our forefathers on the Declaration of Independence just because, as my own child's teacher told me, "Well, everything is done on a keyboard now."

The bottom line is that someone arbitrarily made the decision that we no longer *value* this form of communication. An entire generation lost out on learning what was considered a fundamental skill. Who is deciding what our values are, if it's not us..."we the people"? The digital takeover has now dictated that we also do not value down time, privacy, ending a workday or taking a vacation where we're actually unavailable, among other things. Technology has changed our values, because we allowed it to.

The good news is that history shows us that just like the ever-swinging pendulum, we always seem to find our way back to a life that reflects our very human needs. In the 50s we all moved from the family dinner to the TV trays, shifting from face-to-face interactions to face-to-screen. However, as years went by, television technology got cheaper and cheaper, and everyone had one in their room. The family experience became more and more isolating and there was a call for change. Feeling the need for reconnection, and with research showing the need to "talk to your kids," we saw a call to get back to the table. Public service announcements praised the importance of family time and talking and listening to one another.

Today I'm not seeing that message come across the TV as much as I'm seeing a teenage kid order his robotic companion to send a command to his friends: "Tell [the girls] our band is playing at the garage." He speaks as if he's a power executive, and then commands his feminine robot to only refer to him as "Rock God." How does this behavior shape the "self"? I don't remember a good outcome for the men in *The Stepford Wives.*

In another cell phone commercial during the introduction of and excitement about voice recognition technology on our cell phones, does a young girl really need to ask her robotic companion Siri to "remind me to do this again" in order to spend some quality time with her boyfriend after a cross-country trip? Watching these iPhone commercials makes me ask, "What is Siri doing on this trip with them anyway?" Isn't this supposed to be about bonding together, figuring things out together, looking at a map together, exploring restaurants, asking the locals for what they think is the best BBQ, and having some surprises along the way?

If we are just relying on technology, are we flattening out our human experiences? Shouldn't she be turning to *him* to say, "Let's remember to do this again"? That would make the experience about them..."let *us* remember." They're supposed to be talking to one another. And then there's the commercial that asks, "Did you ever think you'd be asking your car for a restaurant suggestion?" No, I didn't, and maybe I shouldn't.

As simple as it seems, talking and listening to one another are among the most fulfilling and important aspects of our human development. They have a direct correlation to our sense of well-being, self-esteem, self-actualization, self-concept, physical and mental health, and happiness, among other things. Research shows that having just one person in your life to confide in and who will listen to you is an enormous benefit to your self-esteem. Listening is one of the most valuable and transformative behaviors within the human experience, and yet we rarely invest our time and energy into really learning how to listen.

Less then two percent of the population has ever had any formal training in listening. Listening is very different from hearing. Listening is one of the most loving things you can do for someone. If you can listen with patience and empathy, speak to validate, question to clarify or really understand, you will have acquired a fundamental communication skill that is the core to getting your personal needs met and improving your connections and level of happiness and fulfillment. And, no batteries required!

> "I wouldn't say a single word to them, I would listen to what they had to say, and that's what no one did."
> — Marilyn Manson, *Bowling for Columbine*

Since we're taking the time to reevaluate the way we are using technology today, it's important to establish our vision of the human experience. So, what do we value? What do we need? What aspects of our 21st-century digital devices are enhancing those values, and what tools are being used in a way that is eroding them? It's really a pretty simple concept. We just have to use one of our human apps, one that is automatically downloaded and instantly activated when needed. It's called instinct.

Instinct is just one of the bazillion apps that every human being comes with. It pops up all the time. Unfortunately, we keep on clicking the "Ignore this message" button. We might not be using instinct as much as we should, but we're all born with it and can benefit immensely if we quiet the static in the world around us and tune in and quietly connect with ourselves. Sometimes we refer to instinct as our "gut" or "inner voice." Scientific research shows that we have this amazing app that will work for us, even save our lives, if we just listen to it, respond, act on that feeling. It's when we *ignore* instinct that we get into trouble.

Malcolm Gladwell, who is considered one of the greatest thinkers of our generation, explores the science behind that human phenomenon we refer to as our gut feeling in his book *Blink*. In story after story, Gladwell gives remarkable evidence of the incredible human characteristic he refers to as "rapid cognition," the ability to know something in less then two seconds. In the blink of an eye, we look at something and our brain goes to work. Like rapid fire, it spits out answers all day long. Gladwell substantiates the concept of rapid cognition, or the psychological term "thin slicing," with case studies, stories, and statistics of the amazing accuracy of this natural human app. He feels that if we can cultivate and value this aspect of our humanness, we will benefit ourselves and our future.

On his personal website Gladwell says, "I think it's time we paid more attention to those fleeting moments. I think that if we did, it would change the way wars are fought, the kind of products we see on the shelves, the kinds of movies that get made, the way police officers are trained, the way couples are counseled, the way job interviews are conducted and on and on — and if you combine all those little changes together you end up with a different and happier world." Gee, that was easy. So what is it really that we want?

The basic needs of our human existence have never changed. No matter what goes on throughout the world around us, we all share the same basic needs. The greatest minds in the world have been trying to make sense of our human existence. That is the beauty of being a human. We are the most complex species on the planet. Everyone from

Aristotle and Socrates to Freud and Carl Rogers, whose classic psychology book has the manual-sounding title *On Becoming a Person*, has been trying to offer substantial answers as to why we are who we are. The one fundamental rule that seems to transcend time is that the most important part of humanity lies within our authenticity.

> "Experience is, for me, the highest authority. The touchstone of validity is my own experience. No other person's ideas, and none of my own ideas, are as authoritative as my experience. It is to experience that I must return again and again, to discover a closer approximation to truth as it is in the process of becoming in me."
> — Carl Rogers, *On Becoming a Person*

In 2010, a group of young filmmakers explored the idea that our society has forgotten what it means to be human. They captured a 21st-century idea of humanity in their award-winning documentary *The Human Experience*, in which they set out to find some of the common denominators that unite us as people by interviewing everyone from homeless New Yorkers all the way to the lepers of Ghana. What the filmmakers confirm is that we do indeed share the same universal needs. However, what is most interesting is that this group of young filmmakers is representative of a population and movement of young people who feel a strong pull to explore "the meaning of life."

Anthropologists, sociologists, philosophers, psychologists, and just about every human being on the planet ask about meaning and purpose. We now have documentaries like *The Human Experience* and *The Collective Evolution* (parts one and two), created by another group of young filmmakers and asking questions such as "Did we forget what it means to be human?" and are we living "through our hearts afraid to love?" The fact that these are topics for the 18- to 25-year-old demographic may demonstrate that there is a growing need for deeper and more authentic connections.

We have been living through media, through other people's mediated lives, and forgetting to feel what it feels like to have our own authentic experiences of life. We need to feel what it feels like to live a truthful life, genuine to our own values and visions, and not through the visions and experiences of the media makers.

"All the evidence that we have indicates that it is reasonable to assume in practically every human being, and certainly in almost every newborn baby, that there is an active will toward health, an impulse towards growth, or towards the actualization."
— Abraham Maslow

In 1943, Psychologist Abraham Maslow introduced the world to his concept of universal human needs with his "Theory of Human Motivation" paper. It has since become the clearest understanding and most widely-accepted concept of the foundation for our human needs. Maslow used a pyramid to demonstrate that until our most basic physical needs are met, we cannot move up the pyramid.

Obviously, our physical needs are the most important...the basics such as air, water, food...all simple human needs. Once those are met, we can move up to the second level: safety and security...shelter, sense of living in an environment free from physical harm, and financial security, among others.

The third most demanding need is the social level. Humans are social by nature, so behaving in a way to meet these needs is just about as instinctual as our core physical and safety needs. We have to be social, or else the entire species dies. We are not amoebas that split automatically; we are hardwired to seek partners in order to procreate and keep the species going. Among the concepts of the social needs category is what Maslow describes as a need to belong — belonging to social groups, developing relationships such as friendships, family, and romantic attachments.

The fourth area, once the first three fundamental needs are met, is personal worth. We have a need to develop our own self-esteem, validation, recognition, love, and affection. The last area of human needs, which is at the top of the pyramid, is our need for personal growth and self-actualization. This is the area where deeper fulfillment of a spiritual nature can be cultivated.

As we came to know what our needs were, the creative minds of brilliant inventors were motivated to create things that met those needs. Creative advertisers understood that the best way to get people to buy things was to showcase them in a way that underscores people's need, or at least perceived need, for what is being sold. We are lucky to have evolved in a society where we can feel pretty confident about basic needs being met...we have plenty of food, safe water, safe air, pretty safe environments...meaning, we can feel pretty secure that a panther is not going to pounce on us as we're looking for berries to survive. So, the next step is selling our sense of belonging...love, affection, validation, connection. It's pretty easy to sell something that we have a strong desire for, so is it any surprise that the mere promises of instant connectivity went right to our very souls?

I'M JUST TRYIN' TO FIGURE IT ALL OUT

No one is more vulnerable or more highly values the need to belong than a teenager. Adolescence is the toughest time in our development. We are searching for our individualism while at the same time we are desperately trying to "fit in." Nothing is more important to a teen or young adult than belonging, and nothing is more threatening than being an outcast.

> "If I ever go looking for my heart's desire again, I won't look any further than my own backyard; because if it isn't there, I never really lost it to begin with."
> — Dorothy Gale, *The Wizard of Oz*

The pathology of consumer behavior might not be common knowledge, but believe me, there is big money in understanding the psychological workings of human beings and using that information to drive people to buy. We want to be happy, to feel loved, to be validated, and we are told from birth that happiness is just a "thing" away. We're programmed to believe that happiness is somewhere over there, just out of our reach. This isn't one of our best human traits, but it is real; it's in our DNA.

We are hedonists by nature, always seeking pleasure. If I have one, I want two; if I have two, I want three. If I have the iPhone5, I'm just OK until the next one comes out. If I just had...a million dollars, a raise, a lover, a house, a new iPad, those new shoes...then I'd be happy. It's not pretty, but there it is. It's human. And because advertising is a keystone of our economy, and businesses need to produce consumers to keep the cycle going, we are outnumbered.

When we were restricted in our media consumption to television and radio, the government regulated the mass messages. In the early days, the only way you could actually get a license to broadcast was to prove that you were "serving in the best interest of the public." You had to show that you devoted a certain amount of time to non-revenue producing content. Public service announcements provided a small amount toward balance. It was OK to sell stuff as long as you also served the public with information that might benefit them.

In contrast, for the past 20 years of Internet use, we've been in a free-for-all. We seek out the stuff that we want to know about and disregard anything that doesn't interest us, whether it's good for us to know or not. Because there isn't any money to be made cultivating the concept that true happiness is an attitude that lies within you, that happiness and your heart's desires need to come from within, we are conditioned to seek happiness outside ourselves. And since we've been living with the understanding that anything we need or could ever want can be gotten online, that's where we go to find what we need, including happiness, joy, validation, retail therapy, porn, drugs, sex, or anything else we desire.

Understanding human needs and how people think, both the good and bad, has translated into big media money. Understanding that we need to feel validated and "normal" has been the foundation for the rise of social media and reality television. In the wake of the media-created "real people," we can go online or look to reality television to compare and contrast our own lives with those who have capitalized on the hot career of the 21st century, which is being a "brand." All of this has distorted the lives of those who are just trying to be human.

THE WIZARD

In *The Wizard of Oz,* the wizard created his alter ego, the Great and Powerful Oz, out of his own insecurity. He used his technology to put a false face out to the people of Oz so that they would love him, because he didn't think they would care about him as a mere mortal. The Oz character developed into this big phony image, far beyond his mere mortal capabilities.

As part of being human and trying to balance our lives, we've always had to take on different roles. We learned to live within the scope of our "professional" selves and then our "personal" selves. Our roles were clearly defined, and we had the ability to be "on" at work or around other professionals or in public, and then be our most authentic selves around those who love and accept us for all our ridiculous flaws. It has been within that authentic world of being an idiot *and* being loved *and* being accepted that we thrive most.

Today, however, with our heavy use of social media, the boundaries have blended, and so has our confusion of our selves. Research is showing that more and more young adults and professionals are spending enormous amounts of time creating versions of their different "selves," in the footsteps of the Great and Powerful Oz. It can be exhausting living the *two* lives — the professional and the personal.

So, what happens to someone who is living *various* lives, many of which are total lies? I have heard many gay individuals express how living a life that was not authentic, for a long period of time, was not easy. You know who you are on the inside, and yet have to live a lie. So, what is happening to people who look at their Facebook page or online persona, which may have been embellished a bit, and know deep inside, "That's not me." I'm posting pictures of myself so I look like I have the coolest life and I'm putting out the sexy cleavage shots, but it doesn't feel right. Do I even know who I am? How hard is it to juggle all these different roles? Some theories suggest that this is a way to experiment with different identities during development periods. Perhaps time will tell if this practice has been a benefit or an obstacle. It seems like a lot of work.

How 'bout the theory that you are <u>not</u> a *brand,* you are a *person*. We go through life in the process of self-discovery; we change with every experience; we have many different roles. Trying to fit under one label makes us small. Labeling ourselves does not promote growth. The self-absorbed teen today may be someone's savior tomorrow. I'm sorry Donny Deutsch, I know you're branded the advertising guru for the 21st century, but spreading the idea that every*one* is a brand is a confusing message. Particularly for young people who are just trying to figure out how to be a teen, a friend, a person, let alone a "brand." It's dehumanizing.

When you're trying to figure out how to be a human being, it's not fair for you to also have to be a slick image consultant, examining your own online presence as if you were a politician who has to monitor every word and evaluate all photos for release. Then to have to determine if this image that has been painstakingly created matches the image of the "brand" known as "me"? Then you look around to see if anyone is feeling the same way, and it's hard to find any authenticity — everyone is on Facebook protecting their "brand" and their image.

From the beginning of time, as part of the human experience, we have looked to others to figure out how to "be," asking ourselves, "Am I normal?" So, what happens when we're spending time in the social media world, double-checking to see if "I'm normal" if so much of the stuff that we're comparing ourselves to is bullshit?

When we look to television shows, we see the extremes. We see the rich and famous who are bitching over who drank too much Chardonnay or who's flippin' out over cheating husbands. On the other extreme, there are people who are struggling to lose 200 pounds or are fighting some horrific life-altering illness. For most of us, our search for humanness is in the middle. However, just because we're not dealing with extreme issues doesn't mean that we're not in need of understanding and compassion for some basic human questions. So, we seek. The answers have to be somewhere.

"The answer to a lot of your life's questions is often in someone else's face. Try putting your iPhones down every once in a while and look at people's faces. People's faces will tell you amazing things."
Amy Poehler, *Harvard Commencement Speech*, May 25, 2011

In my conversations with people who spend a lot of time on social media, many have said that they use it to "escape." If they're spending time "creeping on friends" or checking out other people's lives, then they don't have to deal with their own. In the movie *The Wizard of Oz*, Dorothy Gale, a typical teenager whose aunt and uncle think she's always getting into trouble, finds herself in the midst of teenage confusion, hoping to find a place where life is easier and not so confusing. This is now social media's role. It's one reason why teens and young adults spend so much time in this other world, a world where they can escape the reality of life during their transformative years.

Hey, what could be better? You can tune out the world around you, leave the pressures of the family, and create a world where it's just you and your cyber friends — while still physically at home or in a dorm room, surrounded by family and friends in the flesh. However, the more time we spend in the cyber world, the less time we spend in the real world and the less opportunity we have to learn to cope with real-world situations. Technology offers an opportunity for escapism. Even though they may be physically under one roof, from a psychological aspect, people are living more isolated lives and are in their own universe.

Back in 2006, *Time* magazine did a feature story on whether our kids are too wired for their own good. The potential risks were on the radar screen back then as we were starting to see the impact of our digitally-focused families. Included in the report was the research from UCLA's four-year study from the Center on Everyday Lives of Families. Researcher Elinor Ochs expressed concern, saying "I'm not certain how the children can monitor all those things at the same time, but I think it is pretty consequential for the structure of the family relationship."

The study observed daily family interactions and, as she concludes, "Everyone is ignoring each other." Ochs explains that it's "hard for parents to penetrate the kid's universe so they end up backing away. This digital abandonment leaves many of these kids 'over there' in this world that can appear fine on the surface; yet you never know what trouble lurks around the corner or what kind of turmoil you might find yourself getting into." The bigger issue here is why we haven't addressed this issue of "digital abandonment." UCLA is as prestigious as they come, and Ochs is highly respected in her field. Yet there has been little media attention on this, and certainly no call to action. The behavior of ignoring each other in the home has spilled over into our society.

Sherry Turkle, who also wrote *The Second Self — Computers and the Human Spirit,* told *Time* Magazine's Claudia Wallis that "Online life is an identity workshop and that's the job of adolescents — to experiment with identity." She has said that she thinks this might be healthy if it's heavily regulated, but that is not happening.

As wonderful as our human traits can be, we have a dark side. We have been sold the concept that technology is to benefit us, bring us together, and offer greater connection. However, because of our human characteristics, like jealousy, judgment, survival, anger, and fear, we have subconsciously allowed certain aspects of technology to amplify these traits. And, because we can release these ugly emotions behind a veil of computer screens, without the personal accountability of another person's immediate reaction, we can get lost in our own bad behavior, which can become habitual before being accountable.

In a British fashion magazine, one of the writers explained that when she gets on Twitter, she turns into a "nasty bitch," insulting everyone's fashion sense and being mean. When I watch the Academy Awards with my friends, the women *and* men, we start judging and commenting from the moment the first star shows up on the red carpet. "Oh my God, what happen to so and so...what the hell is that thing she's wearing...yo, chill on the Botox." It can be a lovely bonding event for us.

This interesting human trait is called *schadenfreude,* which is German for "happiness at the misfortune of others." We get an emotional reward when we can see the flaws in other people. It allows us to relate and feel connected as part of the human race. We also share another quirky human trait: for some reason, bonding over negative things can produce stronger feelings then bonding over positive things. Think about the heightened emotions of an angry crowd. So, when we compare ourselves with other people, we level the human playing field a bit by finding other people's flaws. It's the "no one (human) can be that perfect" syndrome.

It's one thing to hurl insults at the TV screen in the comfort of my living room with my friends, because I'm sure Nicole Kidman will never hear or care whether or not I like her gown. However, when we participate in this exact same human behavior on social media, we forget that people *are* actually hearing us. Because we are looking to make a connection, others start jumping in on the insult bandwagon. That human phenomenon explains why negative statements get so out of hand so fast on Facebook. In one example, a student said she watched helplessly as people were talking about her online. She wanting to just scream "Hellooooo, I'm right here!"

I've interviewed stars in person on the red carpet who were wearing some ugly dresses. However, as you're looking someone in the face, you forget the dress and just share their enthusiasm and their emotional excitement of the moment. On the social media red carpet, where everyone is putting on their best face, you don't experience someone "looking" at you. You don't pick up the social cues that you need in order to influence your behavior.

Try This

See if you can compare the emotional impact of positive comments and negative comments on Facebook and Twitter. Does a negative comment snowball out of control and get more people involved in the dialogue threads than a positive comment? Do people start taking sides? Do little cyber-wars break out?

As humans, we sometimes do things that we're not so proud of. The digital world has a way of amplifying our ugly traits. Things happen so fast and impulsively, and to so many people at once, that by the time we realize what we did or said, it's too late. We get so caught up in the frenzy, the "look-how-low-I-can-go" attention-grabbing behavior, that in a fraction of a second, with one little click, the damage is done.

"Character is doing what's right when nobody's looking."
— J.C. Watts

In the quiet of our own self-reflection, we find ourselves disappointed in our own behavior. It's called "guilt." The internal dialogue starts with "Oh my God, I really must be the biggest bitch," or "Boy, I was really an asshole to say that." This can become a toxic and damaging pattern as young people are shaping their identity. Younger and younger people are communicating meaner and meaner. We're not just talking about the bullying behavior; meanness is creeping into mainstream online communication almost to the point where public humiliation is not only tolerated but accepted as part of the trade-off. It's a pretty dangerous direction when public humiliation becomes a "social norm."

It is important to talk about how we're feeling when we're using social media and digital connections. I know that when I've talked about this in small group settings, I've seen the stunned faces of students expressing some version of "How did you know how I was feeling?" or more importantly,

"Thank God I'm normal." It's important to be human with one another and know that social media can foster negative behavior. At some point we might reach the enlightenment of a Mother Teresa, but until then, if we know about our humanness, the good, the bad and the ugly, and understand how technology can tap into all three areas, we can see the digital world for the good, the bad, and the ugly as well.

We don't openly admit that we need attention. We don't usually say, "Hey everyone, will you all come over so I can host a party so I will get the feeling of being the center of everyone's attention for a while?" Some people need a lot of attention, while others start twitching at the thought of being the center of attention. But as humans, we *all* share the need to be acknowledged by other people.

I have a friend who is a brilliant and talented comedian. For years he did stand-up all over the country. Shortly after I referred him to a friend for a job hosting a morning radio show, which he got, we went out to celebrate. He and his new bride were thrilled that they could finally have a "normal" life — well, as normal as being a radio personality can be. He saw "normal" as being able to give up his "stand-up" life in a club every night. When friends asked him if he was going to miss doing the comedy club thing, he said, "I don't need that now...I'm happy. I only needed that when I needed the love and attention from an audience."

We all need attention. It's the "ego" part of our human psyche's need for validation from others. Yes, *egotistical* comes from the same place and can have a negative connotation. However, we're talking about our essential desire for normal acknowledgment from other human beings. The need for attention is an intrinsic human characteristic.

Individually, we're all born unique in personality, disposition, sensitivity, intelligence, talent, and ability, just to name a few. Then of course, we are shaped by environment, experiences, learned social values, parental guidance, trauma, neglect, love, affection, and support — again, just to name a few. However, we are mostly shaped by our relationships with other people. In psychological and sociological terms, we learn how to "be" by observing members of the social tribe. Modeled behavior is extremely influential in the shaping of individuals. Sometimes we go looking for that in all the wrong places.

Dorothy in *The Wizard of Oz*, like every other teenager, was at that period in her life where she was trying to figure it all out. Adolescence is an extraordinarily confusing time in everyone's life, when we are breaking away from childhood, starting to realize that we are not our parents, and grasping the fact that we are our own person (that in itself is pretty frightening).

We're developing our emotional intelligence and identity. It certainly doesn't help that we have these crazy hormones taking over any sensibility we thought we might have and attacking our minds with all sorts of stuff that make us feel like we must be a total freak of nature because no sane person could possibly be thinking the things we're thinking. Whew!

For those who are currently young adults, it certainly didn't help that this difficult period in their lives coincided with the new digital age, putting them smack in the middle of uncharted territory. Parents and adults could not help them navigate through the emotional and confusing issues of being socialized in a digital world, because they had no experience. When kids told their parents, "You don't understand," for the first time in many generations they were right.

During adolescence, generation after generation has looked to one another for validation that they're not crazy. Characters in books and movies gave us the validation we needed to assure us of our sanity. Or, at least we were able to say, "OK, thank God I'm not that bad." However, characters written for a book, film, or television are the creation of someone's imagination. We know that. We can justify behavior unlike our own because they're "not real." What is different now is that as we look to others on social media sites and even television to figure out how to "be," we are comparing ourselves to fabricated versions of reality, yet being told they're "real" people. That has screwed with the development of our identities.

People who have left the digital planet for a while have had time to examine their own lives. Once they have backed away a bit, they can see how the lure of escapism can be so addictive. Many have told me that they cannot believe how they were "living their lives through the lives of others" or that "I really need to start living my own life."

In follow-up interviews, many young people say they have found more happiness and joy when they are just "with my real close friends" instead of being on social media sites. They say, "That's enough" or "These are the people I *know* *r*eally care about me, everything else is bullshit." It's as though they've been to the crazy world of Oz, and now they're back. Maybe this is just part of the maturing process. It seems like they went wandering, seeking, and found the most happiness "in their own backyard."

We have been trying to figure out this "people" thing for centuries. The process of self-discovery and finding out who we are to others is a part of life itself. We will never have any undeniable answer. Life and humanity will continue to keep us wondering, as humanity in itself remains beautifully mysterious. As part of being human, we will continue to see if somewhere "over the rainbow" is better. We seek to see if anyone else can offer a place, somewhere far, far away, to escape the struggles of finding ourselves. Where we once had "bluebirds" flying over the rainbow, we are now dealing with "angry birds" over the Internet.

> "What a world, what a world, what a world."
> — The Wicked Witch

Chapter 4

The Emotional Cell

> *Apple Inc. is now the largest single company in the world,*
> *with over a billion dollars in annual revenue.*

Our human needs are powerful. They go to our very core of survival — the air, food, and other things we need simply to exist. However, our existential needs are just as necessary to our survival. We need to be loved, to receive affection, to be understood, to create, to be accepted, to understand ourselves, to live with purpose, to experience inner peace and a sense of joy and happiness.

By our very nature, we are hardwired for pleasure. We have cultivated a society in which we are used to getting our pleasures instantly. The digital age has taken instant gratification to a whole new level. We see, we want, we click. Everything from a pizza to porn is right at our fingertips. Our society has been sold on the concept that happiness is getting what we want when we want it.

Understanding the psychological workings of the human being and using that information to drive the person to take action to purchase is a winning formula when it comes to advertising. We always want what we don't have, believing that happiness is just a "thing" away. It's human.

The "thing" of the 21st century is technology. We are spending billions of dollars advertising all the benefits of our digital devices and promising that these devices are the answer to everyone's needs. According to *Forbes* magazine, in 2012 Apple alone spent $933 million on advertising. Industries skyrocket not just because corporations create products that meet our needs, but also because they create products that meet our demand for pleasure.

According to a *Washington Post* report, the food industry spends between $10 and $15 billion on marketing soda and fast food directly targeted to the 2- to 17-year-old demographic. Meanwhile, only $1.6 billion is devoted to healthy eating initiatives. Health advocates have referred to this as "engineered addiction." A "sugar high" is a real thing. Advertising the benefits and joy of eating a tomato off the vine is good for our society; however, it doesn't translate into corporate revenue. Therefore, we have been living on the satiating consumption of refined sugar and fat that gives the body an instant spike — meeting our demand for pleasure.

Dr. Ronald Siegel, a Massachusetts psychologist, writes in his book *The Mindful Solution* that we are "hooked on pleasure." Siegel explains that the tendency to seek pleasure and avoid pain, "while great for our collective survival, locks us into shopping for pleasure and running from pain all day long." Selling pleasure has been a lucrative formula. That's why you see this pattern repeated over and over.

No matter what the product is, the advertiser's job is to create a life-long consumer, brand loyalty, and the perception of need. As we've seen in Maslow's theory, as long as the basic needs are met, the next level is love and connection. The documentary *Consuming Kids* exposes the practice of advertisers "hooking them from birth" to be consumers. During a conversation I had with producer and media scholar Sut Jhali about showing his film in my class, he explained that no matter what the product is, you can "bring it back to selling love." Buying is all emotion based.

In my media literacy class, we turned this into a little game of "three degrees of commercialization." We tied every product into meeting the three human demands for food-water-air, survival-safety-security, and then love-bonding. We discussed long-lasting lipstick, which will make you beautiful to attract someone so you will feel loved. Diet Pepsi, so you will get thin, look like Sofia Vergara, and attract someone so you will be loved. And the new Droid, iPhone5, or latest smartphone that will allow you to always be "connected" with an instant app for Facebook or Twitter, so you will never be alone and you can always feel loved and connected. The mediated message is that you *need* these devices so much that if you *don't* have one, then you *won't* be connected and you *won't* be loved.

Fear is an excellent tool for sales. Think about the brain of an adolescent, who has an overwhelming need for connectivity to friends and peers and at this age believes that friendships are almost more important than food and safety. You can see how the cell phone phenomenon captivated a generation at its most vulnerable time in personal development. For parents, knowing the potential dangers of the adolescent period, the cell phone was a way to keep the connection between parent and child at this time of increased independence. It was embraced as a way to alleviate some of their worries.

Thinking back to Maslow's pyramid, why would we need anything other than a phone that is used as a phone? Well, because that can only connect you to one person at a time. Today's "new need" is being connected to everyone you know, plus all 872 "friends," in case anyone you have ever met needs to get in touch with you. The message is that if you don't have the latest phone — the new status symbol, by the way — or if you're not on Facebook, on Twitter, or playing Angry Birds like everyone else, YOU will be left out, unconnected, lonely, unloved. Maybe for someone who is emotionally mature it might not be such a threat, but for adolescents, it might be something they feel they cannot afford to risk.

MEDIA CONSUMPTION

Media scholar George Gerbner has been studying the effects of violent images and messages in the media on individuals and society for over four decades. From the early days of films, social scientists have been trying to make a connection between watching a violent image and actual violence. However, Gerbner's research finds the opposite. With more and more violent images coming into our living rooms on television crime dramas and news stories, we are more protective of ourselves. The documentary *Mean World Syndrome* demonstrates Gerbner's work. His statistical evidence shows that through mediated messages, news programs, entertainment television, and films, we perceive the world to be a much more dangerous place than it really is. What we know is that violent and fear-evoking media is profitable.

In the early days of Silicon Valley, the young digital pioneers of the 90s planned to create and invent *against* the commercialized mainstream media. However, the combination of ego, power, and money is pretty seductive to even the most ardent technophile, as we have seen with the rise of Google and Facebook. In his best-selling book *You Are Not A Gadget: A Manifesto,* Jaron Lanier, who is considered the father of virtual reality technology, writes, "The centrality of advertising to the new digital hive economy is absurd, and it is even more absurd that this isn't more generally recognized."

As someone who was at the forefront of this explosion and pocketed a lot of money for his own contributions, Lanier is also concerned about the slippery-slope effects on our society. In various interviews, he has talked warmly about the birth of his child, who became his "muse" and opened his eyes to authentic beauty in the perfection of the human, as is. As a writer, musician, and father, Lanier is concerned about the imbalance of values: "If you want to know what's really going on in a society or ideology, follow the money. If money is flowing to advertising instead of musicians, journalists and artists, then a society is more concerned with manipulation than truth or beauty."

At the same time technology is feeding the ravenous pleasure-seeking demands of our society, there is an emerging love/hate relationship going on with our devices and social media.

> "All this digitalizing world we're in, it really does suck.
> I mean, I really just feel like a number."
> — Joey, 15

There seems to be a sense of being used.

It's not that we should object to all forms of advertising. We like to know what's available to us to bring us pleasure or serve our needs. The problem is when advertising goes beyond serving a need and we start to get that feeling of "OK, now you're just using me." And there is the ever-growing "creep factor" as the Internet tracks your purchases, your Facebook "likes," and your Google searches in order to profile and target you as the perfect consumer for specific products.

IBM reports that in the next five years, the online profile of users will be so precise that we'll never have to deal with spam because "they'll know" your exact wants and needs. Advertisers will be able to micro-target their persuasive messages. Is this serving *us,* or are the companies just trying to sell products? In other words, we can look at this from two different perspectives. Yes, it's easy to find what you want, but look how easy it is for companies to find you.

For years, grocery stores have put small items near the checkout area for impulse sales. They're there at your fingertips. Your kid is holding a bag of M&M's, jumping up and down and screaming, "Please, please, can I have M&M's ...can I have some gum...can I have these Tic Tacs...please, please." And because the items are right there, we cave in. And on the Internet, because what we want is right there and we can just click the credit card account, we click.

> The most frequent Facebook users are aged 18 to 34, according to the Reuters 2012 survey, with 60 percent of that group being daily users.

When enough is enough, people will stop financially supporting companies whose business policies show a callous disregard for them as humans by tapping into their fears. Ultimately, consumers can send the message that we deserve respect, and businesses need us more than we need them. Keep in mind that many companies use focus groups to get feedback for making policy changes and conceptualizing their campaigns.

If you watch commercials closely these days, you might be seeing a trend toward more personal service and a more human touch. Ally Bank uses a spot in which a person has been replaced by a machine. (People walk into a dry-cleaning store and they're confronted by a blender on the counter in place of a person.) The announcer says, "We found that people didn't like that very much. So, at Ally, we believe in people sense." Chase Sapphire Blue credit card is also jumping on the personal service trend. Their spot features a man at a rental car desk sounding as if he was a phone recording: "Press one for... at Chase..." Chase now provides a real person to talk to 24/7.

BUYER BEWARE

Facebook is officially on record with the New York Stock exchange as a data collection corporation. Facebook does not fall under any of the traditional guidelines for a broadcast medium, although it is a form of mass communication. You need to understand the deal that you're making with Facebook and what the tradeoff is. Facebook allows you to use their digital airwaves to exchange information and market yourself and/or your goods and services, in exchange for Facebook collecting and owning your personal information in order to sell you, in data form, to advertisers.

Facebook's value on the stock exchange is based on its assets, which are the Facebook users. According to a *Wall Street Journal* online article by researcher Doug Laney, who made some calculations based on Facebook's S-1 filings, "You are worth about $81 to Facebook. Your 'friendships' are worth $0.62 each, and your profile page could be valued at $1,800. The value of a business page is worth approximately $3.1 million." Laney writes, "Put another way, Facebook's nearly one billion users have become the largest unpaid workforce in history." Maybe this is why it is getting the nickname *Facecrook*?

As of June 2012, a survey shows that Facebook use is declining and that Facebook is having big problems turning use into dollars for advertisers. According to the study results from Reuters, "Four out of five Facebook Inc. users have never bought a product or service as a result of advertising or comments on the social network site." And, just so you have fair warning, the Reuters/Ipsos poll goes on to suggest that "much more needs to be done to turn its 900 million customer base into advertising dollars."

Some companies take the karmic approach: serve the customer in a spirit of respect and genuine service, and you will be rewarded. Treating people like people and honestly "connecting" on a personal level can have solid economic benefits.

Here's a little side story.

I had to call the Black & Decker customer service line for a replacement part that was out of warranty. I got a lovely woman on the phone, but I could tell from her voice that she wasn't so thrilled; she was just reading through the script. So, I asked very genuinely, "Really...how are you doing today?" She seemed to be surprised that I had shifted from obscure customer to real person. As we chatted a bit, I heard all about her problems with an aging mother, the pressures that can have on a family, and how the weather was, and we "shared" a few little laughs. She took a minute to take care of my business, made an exception for me by sending me the $12.00 part, and said, "I have to tell you, you really made my day. I can't remember the last time someone actually asked me how I was doing...and I really needed that today."

Maybe that took an extra five minutes — just five minutes out of my entire day. So ask yourself, how many "five minutes" do I waste on some Internet time-suck or cell phone game or online shopping, while making an excuse that I don't have time for people? In the grand scheme of life, what matters more?

Try This
Spend just one day being mindful about how much time you spend looking at stuff, being exposed to ads online. How much time do you spend making self-serving connections? Compare that to how much time you spend being cordial to those who are serving you throughout the day, or who need just five minutes of your time.

Chapter 5

The Cost of Convenience

"You can choke on the good stuff too."
— Dr. Steven Freilich, Psychologist

Sometimes, pleasurable stuff can make you sick. The sugar rush feels good for a while, or that greasy burger and fries are super tasty. The two bottles of wine take all the pain away, at least for a while. We can choke on the good stuff as well as the bad, and as humans, we are no strangers to over-consuming or turning a blind eye to what we know might not be good for us. We're willing to pay the price because the quick fix, convenience, and pleasure outweigh any long-term consequences.

Try This

Think about the last time you were out partying. How many times did you stop to *think* about the hangover you were going to have the next day? Or, when you were in the middle of a drunk dial, did you stop to *think* about the consequences? Circle one: Yes / No

---

Sometimes what starts out as a good idea goes overboard, and then we need to backpedal and make adjustments. For instance, if you drive a car to work every day and have a sedentary job, you need to balance that with a trip to the gym or some form of exercise. Studies find that the best way to ward off the mentally debilitating effects of Alzheimer's disease is to keep the brain active by playing mentally exercising games like Sudoku, playing an instrument, or reading in order to keep the brain "sharp." Yet we cave in to the convenience of Googling everything, or asking Siri, without giving ourselves two minutes to actually *think.* If we are going to continue to use "smart" technology, we might have to incorporate some compensatory strategies in order to keep our minds from turning to mush.

Whenever there is a digital gain, we have to recognize the human losses. Every time a machine does something that a human used to do, we end up loving the convenience without ever calculating the side effects.

Erika, fashion student, August 2012

"Since I've been in this class and we've been talking about this stuff, I'm really conscious of these things now. Like the other day, I went to the bank and decided I would actually go up to the teller. When I walked in, I saw that there was a line at the ATM and only one teller at the one open window. There was nobody in line for the tellers. There were all these empty windows at the bank where there used to be a person that you could interact with. It really made me kinda sad and I thought it was a good example of how we are losing those little daily opportunities to interact with a real person."

Historically, as modern conveniences have come into our lives, we have tended to embrace them immediately, live with them to see how they fit into our society, and finally think about the costs. Have we lost things that we can afford to abolish from our world, or are we losing things that we still value and need to find ways to hold onto? Hindsight is 20/20, and sometimes we don't feel the consequences until it's too late. We are now trying to reverse the effects of our drive-through food culture of the past three decades. So, what are the consequences of our supersized digital cosumption? What is the cost of all our 21st-century connectivity and communication conveniences?

Anthropologists understand that if you want to know about a society, you need to examine how the people communicate with each other. What do you think you'd conclude if you were visiting this culture for the first time and watched contemporary communication behavior? The general consensus during classroom and casual conversations on this topic is that "People are ignoring one another." It seems we are living in a world of distorted reality; we end up living through media and not through natural and personal interactions.

In 1934, when movies had become part of the entertainment world, social scientist H.J. Forman wrote *Our Movie Made Children*. Forman's book monitored the effects of films and their content on the children of that era. When television entered our homes in the 50s, couches that had once been set up to face each other for socializing were now switched around to face the new television screen. Kids of the 60s and 70s, most of the parents of the Millennials, had to deal with their parents' fear that sitting too close to the television would "ruin our eyes." They were constantly being scolded and told "Don't sit so close to the TV."

The amount of viewing time wasn't a huge concern, since the lack of children's programming (cartoons were reserved for Saturday mornings only) resulted in built-in viewing limitations. As soon as the last cartoon was over, the TV was turned off and the kids were kicked out the door. As cable emerged in the 80s and there was a greater demand for more and more networks, including 24/7 children's shows, television became a convenient babysitter. Countless research studies poured into the public mainstream about the negative effects of kids watching too much television.

Despite decades of studies showing the correlation between increased television watching and negative health for both kids and adults, the seduction of the medium continues to outweigh its proven ill effects. The convenience of instant food and instant entertainment has ushered in a new generation of sedentary kids, more obese and less health-conscious. By the 90s, video games on home computers and continuously improving TV game platforms occupied kids and adults for hours and hours of nonstop mental stimulation. Kids playing video games in front of a TV for hours after school with their friends was the new norm. And in the latchkey era of the 90s, parental oversight and enforcement of limits were new challenges.

Researchers produced study after study of the long-term effects of nonstop screen time, with its resulting lack of physical activity and social interactions. And yet, behavior didn't change. In fact, as we are seeing today, parents who once vowed that they would never let their kids watch TV all day long are now driving around in their minivans (living rooms on wheels) with pop-down movie screens for their infants, even though it has been widely reported that the American Academy of Pediatrics discourages media consumption before the age of two.

According to "experts" on the PBS parent website, parents should be conscious that every minute of screen time is a minute that a child is not engaging in face time. However, the same "experts" don't see a problem with preschoolers having time on iPads and say that smartphones and tablets are appropriate for 11-year-olds, as long as they are kept out of the bedroom. Really? 11?

So the question is, what happened to the social values that were once part of our lives? Do we no longer value the importance of personal interaction, face time, engaging in the world around us, dinner conversation with kids, or listening to the imaginative ramblings of two five-year-olds in the back seat of a car who have to use their own personal creative apps to entertain themselves?

Are children always supposed to be pacified and kept quiet with some form of flickering digital image to keep them distracted? And what are we distracting them from? Coping with the world around them? Are we supposed to hand a smartphone to every fidgety toddler or allow every bored 10-year-old to spend hours face-to-screen, scrolling through the latest apps on their own smartphones?

Every time a society embraces new technology, it has to be prepared to experience some unforeseen and perhaps un-intended consequences. We have been living with the ulti-mate conveniences of the digital age, the infinite information of our Google world, 24/7 personal connectivity, and the "apps for everything" decade. Have we stopped to think about what all this is costing us in the way of our minds, bod-ies, and souls? It may be more than we thought.

92   Celling Your Soul

Chapter 6

Unintended Consequences

For over two decades we've been living with the Internet, first stationary and now mobile, and we have seen some of these unintended consequences, both physical and mental. Nicholas Carr's *The Shallows: What the Internet Is Doing to Our Brains* is a highly acclaimed bestseller that describes the effects of technology on our brains, including the decline in linear thinking ability, depth of thought, and attention span, as well as the effects of instant information. Yet despite his superb research, and all the supportive research since the release of his book, we continue to justify the continuous *limitless* use of today's technology. If behavior is the most accurate form of communication, we are saying that these negative effects are appropriate trade-offs and acceptable collateral damage for the greater good.

We know media shapes us. But how exactly is the digital evolution of media transforming us, individually and as a society? We have become obsessed. The degree of obsession depends on the person, but we can no longer deny what we saw coming for a long time. It is truly time for a reevaluation; time to ask ourselves, as our heads are focused on the screen, what parts of our human experience did we allow to slip away?

What started out as just another form of media intended for greater convenience, productivity, information, and peace of mind turned into a global dependency. When the smartphone went mainstream, the 24/7 digital life changed us immeasurably. It transformed the way we think, feel, interact, communicate, and navigate through the world. It changed our values, our work ethics, our minds, the way we operate, the way we think and feel about ourselves, and the way we relate to others. We didn't see all this coming. The technology was just too cool.

As cool and intriguing as these new devices have been, over the past decade we started to see some alarming behavior that was the impetus for massive studies.

THE OBSESSION

It's easy to see how we have become obsessed with our digital devices and the "wow factor" of the past couple of decades of changing technology. What we can do with them and how we can use them baffles even the most dedicated techie. Over these past six years, while working with young adults who have been socialized in the digital age, I observed student after student struggling with the idea and then the challenge of being without their phones for even a short amount of time.

February 2007

"OK, cell phones are to be turned off and put away," I announced, as was the new routine for just about every class I started. "You guys can focus for at least an hour," I continued. As I was getting ready to start the Interpersonal Communication class, I noticed that one girl was clutching her phone with a look of sheer terror on her face as she continued to text a message.

I stood next to her, asking, "What are you doing?" Without looking up at me, she explained, "I have to text my boyfriend so that he will know I'm in class. I have to let him know that if he doesn't get a message from me it's because I'm in class."

Since this was a teachable moment about communication, I explained that "If he doesn't get a text, just by the fact that he did not get a response from you and he knows that you're at school, isn't that in itself sending the message that you're not available?" As I was explaining this, she was totally obsessed with getting the message to him.

It was actually a bit scary to see this level of desperation and anxiety. I said, "Let me have your phone." She was now just staring at the screen waiting to see the response and not even looking at me. "Seriously, let me have your phone." She handed me the phone and I slid it into the back pocket of my jeans. I continued with the class; however, my real purpose was to observe her behavior and monitor her feelings about being separated from her phone. She could not concentrate or think about anything other than that phone.

"OK, so I'm thinking that none of you can think about anything else other than whether my ass is going to ring, am I right?" Everyone of course started laughing and offering comments to the student like, "Oh my God, I feel your pain" and "I'm dying for you!" I turned to the anxious student and asked, "Are you OK?" She was visibly upset and said, "No, no I'm not, this is killing me." I handed her back her phone and she immediately checked for a response.

"Well?" we were all wondering. "No, nothing…he didn't send me back a text." My first thought was, my God, that was a lot of drama. My next thought was that if I were doing a psycho-logical intake and she was a patient, I'd probably be thinking along the lines of obsessive-compulsive disorder (OCD) or even wondering whether she was dealing with some form of control abuse from her boyfriend. However, because so many other students were relating strongly to her compulsive need to have her phone and expressing an overwhelming sense of "I feel your pain" in regard to her *need* to text her boyfriend, I took this as an early example of how our new technology was conditioning our behavior.

These changes in our social behavior were happening everywhere. Our phones, which used to be sitting at a desk far away from a meeting, or at the bottom of a backpack in case of an emergency, were now front and center. For those of us born before the 1980s, this new behavior appeared to be "just crazy." How could "they" be so obsessed with their phones? Yet, as a society, we were not only accepting the "crazy" behavior, we were actually selling it.

In the Virgin Mobile "Brad & Kelsey" ad campaign, the tag line was "Go crazy with Android." These were "stalker" TV commercials in which Kelsey, after "the best first date," sat in a tree watching Brad's every move. In the next series of the campaign, she showed up in his closet. (I would give you URLs for these; however, Virgin Mobile blocked them from the Internet.) When these ads came out, I used them in class to analyze the mediated message. Students volunteered comments along the lines of, "I know a girl just like that," with other girls saying, "Oh my God, that's actually how *I feel*!" Again, my view was that if this *behavior* were professionally analyzed, poor Kelsey would be in weekly therapy sessions and would probably be put on some meds for psychiatric disorders.

> *64% of the Millennials and 62% of the iGeneration check their technologies every 15 minutes or less (most saying "all the time"), and 51% of both groups get moderately or highly anxious when they can't check as often as they would like.*
> iDisorder, *2012*

It's scary that behavior that was only a few years ago identified as "crazy" and obsessive is now accepted as part of our everyday world. We have to question, is our actual sanity one of the unintended casualties of the digital age?

"I got in the elevator the other day and every single person was using their phones." [referring to face to screen use, not talking]
— Matt Lauer, *The Today Show*, April 2013

Studies are now being released that substantiate what most of us have been seeing and feeling: our digital devices have an addictive component. The research in the July 2012 *Newsweek* magazine *iCrazy* issue was hard to dispute. The issue featured research from more than a dozen countries reporting that *connection addiction* is rewiring our brains and causing not just obsessive behavior, but actual forms of depression and psychosis.

The magazine cited a 2010 study at Stanford University that confirmed what I had been witnessing since 2006. "One in 10 iPhone users feels fully addicted to his or her phone, all but six percent admitted some level of compulsion, while three percent won't let anyone touch their phone."

Going a step further, renowned technology psychologist Dr. Larry Rosen gathered his team of researchers together to conduct studies comparing the behavior of those obsessed with various forms of technology to the measures for diagnosing mental disorders. He coined the term "iDisorder," which is also the name of his book, which tries to make sense of all the new maladaptive symptoms and behaviors that are directly connected to technology.

THE ADDICTION

We hear it all the time: "I'm so addicted to my phone!" Many schools have been trying experiments in which they ask kids to give up their technology for even one day. Just the fact that they often cannot conduct these experiments because kids refuse to participate reveals the level of addiction. *Newsweek* writer Tony Dokoupil explains one problem that I have seen in my own classes. According to the University of Maryland, "Most college students are not just unwilling, but functionally unable, to be without their media links to the world."

Is this really an addiction, like alcohol, sugar, gambling, or crack? Or is it just a bad habit? It's interesting that many substance addicts have mastered the art of denial. The alcoholic or smoker usually says something along the lines of "I can quit anytime I want to, I just don't want to."

However, with technology, the addiction is laughed off with a chuckle or is even considered a badge of honor and rewarded. A teen from Sacramento received news coverage for hitting over 300,000 text messages in just a month. Her mother didn't see anything dangerous about the behavior, since she was a straight "A" student. Neither did the teen, who said to the reporter, "What can I tell you, I'm popular."

> "Nobody can tell me that this isn't a real addiction.
> I know how I feel."
> — Taylor, Photography Major, 2013

However, technology addiction is not a laughing matter. As I have sat with students one on one, they have revealed that they are actually feeling "sick." They aren't sleeping, because they find themselves checking their phones all night long. They can't focus on tasks, because every buzz is a distraction from whatever they're working on. They cannot resist the pull of the technical interaction.

"I have to admit that when I got your email to meet, I almost cancelled. I thought you were going to yell at me for my phone use" explained Taylor, a pink-haired photography major. Taylor had done a class photo project based on her "relationship" with technology, and I reached out to her to see if she'd like to display some of those photos in a gallery show I was doing. "I felt so much better after we met that you really understood what I was going through" she continued. It was during that first conversation that Taylor explained that it took her almost a month during her counseling sessions to get her therapist to see that what she was feeling was not just a habit of our contemporary communication, but that it was a real issue that needed to be addressed professionally. "I feel like I can now finally say, 'I have a problem.' I'm working on it, but I have a problem" she said.

Whether habit, compulsion, or addiction, the behavior is often mindless, and when we are in the habit of doing anything mindlessly, we can get into trouble.

THE BRAIN

Our brains are more amazing than any piece of manmade technology. We have been saying for decades that we haven't even begun to tap into the human brain's potential. If the latest iPhone boasts more than a half a million apps, the human brain can provide millions. What we know now, after decades of research, is that the human brain is malleable. Cognitive therapists and researchers have found that the brain itself can be reshaped by behavior. In other words, not only does the mind grow on what it is fed, but the brain is also shaped physiologically by our behavior.

Thanks to the benefits of modern technology, neuroscientists can actually monitor activity by watching brain scans light up during certain behaviors. For the first time, technology has showed that Internet addicts have the same brain chemistry as drug and alcohol addicts have. In one study, Chinese researchers found abnormal white matter in the brains of those who admitted they feel addicted to technology. It looked like the same physiological characteristics as people who had a clinical addiction to alcohol. The study states, "IAD (Internet Addiction Disorder) may share psychological and neural mechanisms with other types of substance addiction and impulse control disorders."

> *300 million people are online in China, and 24 million have clinical signs of physical addiction. The country is focused on addressing the issue with rehab facilities known as Internet Addiction camps.*

Because this is such a huge issue in China, the problem has been the focus of many studies, all of which reached the same conclusion. Dr. Karen Von Deneen, a professor at Xidian University, has also been examining brain scans of people who are considered Internet addicted and explains, "You would see cognition impairment." Cognition impairment affects the working memory.

The average age of the 24 million Chinese people who are addicted to the Internet is 17, and most are male. Dr. Von Deneen explains that this impairment in working memory means they do not "remember if they ate breakfast." Their brains are actually rewired to ignore basic daily needs; instead, they are wired for one motivation, which is to get on the Internet and "play, play, play."

Even though the Chinese study was reported on major news outlets, including FOX, CNN, and local news stations, these findings didn't seem to provoke the slightest blip of social concern. The horror stories surrounding this physical addiction are numerous and frightening: young adults in Internet café game rooms in China who died because they played for days or months barely eating; a young adult who killed someone for getting in his way; the couple who allowed their biological child to die because they were too busy caring for a "virtual baby." All these issues are "not our problem." Are we able to justify anything that we really want, despite the facts?

Because technology is a new frontier in addiction, there is a lot to explore and learn. For experts in the area of substance addiction, such as alcohol, there is the tangible element of consumption. We have come to learn that the alcohol itself has a rewiring effect on the brain, affecting judgment and resulting in a vicious cycle for the alcoholic, who can no longer use logic to get into treatment. We also know that there are varying degrees, from compulsive drinking to full-blown alcoholism. We know that certain people are predisposed to addiction. However, because technology cannot be poured into a glass or inhaled, we believe it is somehow less consumable.

What exactly are we dealing with here in regard to technology addiction? Just as telling an alcoholic to have only one glass of wine might not work, it might be impossible to tell people who have already moved into full-blown Internet or technology addiction to check their phones just once a day. (I bet even the thought of that might have made you twitch a little.)

SOCIAL SKILLS

Early research reported that video games were beneficial to brain stimulation, peripheral vision, and coordination. UCLA neuroscientist Gary Small, who released his research in his book *iBrain* and is featured in the documentary *Crackberry'd,* said "Searching online actually triggers neurocircuitry, really activates the brain, and may even be a form of brain exercise."

> *The American Academy of Pediatrics discourages media use for children under the age of two specifically because of how it shapes the brain, and for kids older than two, recommends no more than an hour per day and only at 20-minute intervals.*

On the other hand, Small explained, the rewired brain that excels in technological skills shows a loss in the area of the brain that is responsible for social skills. The brain can be highly developed to master technology; however, it becomes underdeveloped in the area of emotional intelligence and recognizing social cues such as facial expressions and emotions. "We know that if the brain spends a lot of time on a particular mental task, over and over again, it will be strengthened, the neurocircuits controlling that task will be very strong. On the other hand, if we avoid certain tasks, the neurocircuits controlling those tasks will be very weak."

We're seeing evidence of this condition on campuses all over. According to a *Men's Health* magazine article, "Today's college kids are the most technologically connected in history. They're also the most socially stunted." The article cites research from the book *Getting Wasted* explaining that social awkwardness may be one of the reasons binge drinking has increased by 75% over the past decade, and with deadly results.

Social skills are developed over time. Let's use our common sense: if you spend more time in front of a screen instead of a person, you simply don't have enough practice time with human interaction, and your brain actually fails to develop social skills to the point where they can be called into service when needed. We can casually joke that the iGeneration will be a generation of socially awkward individuals, or we can recognize the research and learn from history that a steady diet of unhealthy consumption, whether alcohol, sugar, texting, or video games, can have major health implications.

MULTITASKING

We can't. Students will say that they can write a paper while checking Facebook and texting a few dozen friends, with the TV on in the background. The research now indisputably shows that all these things might get done; however, there will be errors along the way. The human brain simply cannot handle the demands of modern-day expectations. As Small explains, "There is a perception that we're getting more done, but we're actually sloppy." We think we are getting a lot done; however, it's all being done half-assed. Or as it's explained by researchers, we're "paying partial continuous attention to many tasks," stressing us out. As we're reminded in the *Crackberry'd* documentary, "Stress can shrink the brain."

Male student, IC class, 2009

"I was trying to buy a car with my brother. I had my phone on and in my pocket when my friend kept texting me. He didn't know I was busy 'cus I just responded to his 'what's up' or whatever. I thought I could just continue texting him, but I was trying to listen to the sales guy, and my friend just kept texting me. I didn't even realize it, but I actually texted him SHUT THE FUCK UP! It's like, that was the thought in my head, and it just came out my thumbs. I really felt bad."

Gary Small explains that the problem is being able to shift from one task to the other, saying "The ability for the brain to switch from task to task might just be microseconds, but that adds up." He explains that every time we switch from one thing to another, the brain has to go through the process of "reorientation." This takes time and uses up our brain's resources. And therefore, we are not as productive as we think we are.

OUR MENTAL HEALTH

We are stressing ourselves out trying to keep up with the pace of a machine, which is humanly impossible. According to reports from China to California, our overloaded human brains are ready to implode. We continue to see research correlating our overuse of technology with impulsivity, stress, anxiety, OCD, ADHD, depression, mood disorders and suicidal thinking. And yet we continue to battle man against machine. Do we aspire to be data-collecting robots? Haven't we seen enough movies about robots wishing they could be *us*, with the capacity for love, understanding, nurturing, compassion, and all those other nice human traits?

Research shows that our digital world is killing us. Psychiatrist Elias Aboujaoude from Stanford University tells *Newsweek* reporter Tony Dokoupil in the *iCrazy* issue, "There's just something about the [digital] medium that's addictive. I've seen plenty of patients who have no history of addictive behavior or substance abuse of any kind become addicted via the Internet and these other technologies." His research reveals a rise in OCD (Obsessive Compulsive Disorder) and an astounding 66% increase in ADHD (Attention Deficit Hyperactivity Disorder).

We are now giving credit to early studies that linked Web use with depression, as more and more studies have substantiated earlier findings. Dokoupil's *Newsweek* report includes results from various studies. Research from Carnegie Mellon shows that "Web use often displaces sleep, exercise, face-to-face exchanges," and Case Western Reserve University reports the correlation between "heavy texting and social media use with stress, depression and suicidal thinking." Even an MTV poll of 13- to 30-year-olds showed, as Dokoupil writes, that they "felt defined by what they put online, exhausted by always having to be putting it out there, and utterly unable to look away for fear of missing out." Or, as we now refer to it, "FOMO."

THINK!

We're not.

Research at MIT revealed a change in student work over the past few years. Papers seem to be written in short bursts of thought, without any long reflection or continuation of linear thought. This has been the major concern of technology scholar Nicholas Carr. He has been writing on the subject for years, asking "Does Google make us stupid?" while being challenged on his philosophy and research by technology advocates.

Carr clearly sees the benefits of the digital world. He explains that the practice of daily technology interaction can increase our ability to take in visual stimulation and multisensory data. However, this ability comes at a cost. "What we lose is the ability to pay deep attention to one thing for a sustained period of time...to filter out distractions."

Carr is concerned that we are sacrificing the part of the brain that serves us in our most human experiences. We are rapidly losing the physiological ability to process deeper thoughts in the way of reflection, contemplation, and introspection. These are the areas that help us solve our problems, build our memories, and store short-term experiences into long-term memory. Carr explains that our ability to focus is our "distinctly human way of thinking." Focus allows us to "build a rich intellectual life." He believes that the Web and the digital world are "pushing us all in the direction of skimming...without allowing us the opportunity to think."

Nobody is saying that we need a world where we are all sitting on a mountain practicing to be great contemplatives. But actually "thinking" should be considered one of the greatest values in the human experience. Unfortunately, our values have shifted from thinking to reacting without thought, collecting data instead of building knowledge.

In an interview with *The Sun,* Carr was asked to respond to the idea that those in the technical world believe technology is about being productive. Carr explained, "I guess it comes down to what you value about human intelligence and, by extension, human culture. Do you believe that intelligence is a matter of tapping into huge amounts of information as fast as possible...or do you think intelligence means stepping back from that information, thinking about it, and drawing your own conclusions in a calm, thoughtful way? My own feeling is that I'd rather have less information and more thoughtfulness. I certainly want information, but information isn't an end unto itself. Human intelligence is the ability to make sense of that information."

Everything is a trade-off. Our brains have been adapting to the nonstop collection of information, data, and visual stimulation. But at some point, we have to decide if it's worth holding on to the ability to process our introspective thoughts, to problem solve, reflect, ponder, understand deeply, critically analyze, imagine, create, and connect those thoughts and ideas in a linear fashion.

HOW MUCH AM I SUPPOSED TO KNOW?

In a recent class exercise, I printed out the home pages of Google, Yahoo, and AOL, reviewing all the headline stories that someone had deemed newsworthy. They ranged from details of the cannibalism drug addict incidents to Fergie's bikini body and Reese Witherspoon's plunging neckline. These were in big, bold letters. In contrast, the world news stories on terrorism were in tiny print.

So, we had a class discussion. Of all these stories, what am I supposed to know? How much of this do I want to consume? Have I already consumed more than I wanted to, just by skimming the front page? How do I really get the information that I should know, if I'm just clicking on the stuff that interests me?

Author Clay Johnson says in his book *The Information Diet* that Americans are now "information obese." Johnson writes, "We have industrialized agriculture, and that's made companies have a fiduciary responsibility to create a cheap and popular food, and we've also industrialized media and that's made it so that companies have to produce cheap and popular information." The author feels strongly enough to call this "a public health problem."

The concept of media as a consumer item is not new. In fact, the whole idea of Media Literacy is about learning to become a more discerning consumer of mediated messages. I've been using a three-bowl approach to teach how to differentiate the massive amount of information we take in. The first bowl is for messages that we sense are good for us, or "healthy" media consumption. Maybe the source is a credible writer or publication, or Pulitzer prize-winning author. The stuff that goes in the "junk food" bowl is pretty easy to recognize. Usually the first thing that we end up writing next to that bowl is "Jersey Shore." No offence,

Snooki, it is what it is and it's not considered a "guilty pleasure" for nothing.

The bowl in the middle contains content that is the most difficult to categorize. I've used an analogy of a granola bar or yogurt. Your first reaction is, "Hmm, it's got oats and nuts," but then you read the ingredients more closely and find out that it contains an enormous amount of brown sugar. Certain forms of media require the consumer to examine the content more closely to understand what we're taking in. For example, entire networks are devoted to "advocacy journalism" programs. The viewer is getting news and information delivered by a powerful personality who is sitting at a news desk. However, there is an underlying biased agenda in the information. Just the words "advocacy journalism" are an oxymoron.

MIT's Media Lab is now working on software that will classify news stories without us *having* to think. Matt Stempeck and his group of researchers are working on a Media Meter, where the idea is "to attempt to automate classification of the topics of individual stories, and then analyze the aggregate. This will give us a sense of how many stories are published about each topic, as well as their frequency and where they appear."

Then, we'll be able to calculate what we're really taking in.

Can we please give humans and our human capacity a little credit? Given the proper *education*, we can tell a credible news story from a piece of crap the same way we can tell a bowl of organic carrots from a bowl of Cheetos.

Chapter Seven

Y

"I'm so fucked up." I can't tell you how many con-versations I've had with students that started with that open-ing line. It seems that our class topic on interpersonal communication strategies, especially regarding intimacy, has hit a chord on some level and requires personal follow-up.

After this class, students' communication manners are refreshingly polite as they use some of the suggested lan-guage to reserve some personal time. "Excuse me, Professor, would you mind if I talk to you for a minute after class?" Then, they get into their emotional dilemma, with a typical line like "Oh my God, I'm so fucked up, I can't believe I..." and explain how they texted something that was taken out of context or posted something stupid on Facebook that was totally misunderstood and took on a life of its own, and then tried to resolve the miscommunication with frantic backped-aling follow-up messages, just making things worse.

Or they thoughtlessly posted a picture, which was then copied and posted on someone else's wall, so that even if they wanted to delete it, they were no longer able to. They feel like victims of their own stupidity. "You can't even make a mistake anymore," one student explained.

I understand that this is the demographic of heightened dramatics in parental disputes, friendships, and romances. But even when students know *intellectually* that they should not be on Facebook so long, or check their texts and phones every two seconds, or impulsively post or tweet and text, the pull is too strong. They admit, "I hate it. I hate that I feel like I have to answer every message or I'll get yelled at," or "I hate that I find myself trying to research something for homework and find myself drifting over to Facebook," or "Oh, I know I'm addicted, there's no doubt."

The thing is, they want to know **why.** Why, with all these so-called "advancements," are they finding themselves with bigger issues — unhappy, confused, feeling unfulfilled in their relationships, and being more "misunderstood" than they feel they should? As with all generations, part of that is just being human and maturing, but part of it is how we are living in our world today.

It's incongruous. We constantly receive information about how devices and social media are "connecting" us, yet that's at odds with how we're really feeling. We see cell phone commercials aimed at making us believe that a device is all you need to bring people together; we watch people with their fabulous lives on Facebook, adding "friends" to see a total tally that rivals attendance figures at Yankee stadium; we make daily observations of people talking and texting.

If this is the way everyone is communicating, and everyone seems to be doing fine, why do *I* feel so disconnected and more alone? The problem is that nobody wants to admit that "lonely" feeling for fear of being branded a loser or, more importantly, damaging the image of the "brand" that they have painstakingly created through social media in order to achieve the love, affection, and validation of others. The simple truth is that we need to nurture *personal interactions* in order to build self-esteem, develop self-confidence, and enrich the spirit. Personal fulfillment has to be done on a personal level.

Despite what technology may promise us, we cannot rely and depend on technology for what is an inherent part of the human experience. Just as we want to believe that a magic pill will give us the bodies we crave with little effort, we also want to believe that our devices and technology will give us the relationships and happy life we want without putting effort into our relationships.

Our emotional health and the success of our relationships require and deserve as much attention and energy as our physical health. We are being told that devices and social media are ways to connect. It's true; they can be — but only on a superficial level. The inner fulfillment that we crave and need as humans in order to thrive and enrich our personal lives can only be achieved when there is authentic intimacy, which requires trust, and building trust requires time.

"Facebook depression" is now a real concern. Think about how the stick-figure images of young girls in fashion magazines and rail-thin movie stars on the red carpet have contributed to an epidemic of body image issues. In the same way, the constant feed of "friends" posting fun, exciting images of their happy lives, regardless of whether they're true or not, leaves users with a feeling of being "less-than" or not "normal" because their lives don't look like that.

An Israeli study at the University of Haifa showed an increased level of anorexia among female Facebook users, who are trying to look as thin as their "friends." The study showed that Facebook images of "friends" had the same type of negative body image influence as television, music videos, and the fashion industry. Even when we logically know that images in magazines are Photoshopped and airbrushed, we still compare ourselves to them. It's just what we do as humans — we look to others to figure out how to "be." It's no surprise that there is an increasing level of low self-esteem and depression for both Millennials and the iGeneration. The study also revealed that youngsters whose parents were directly involved, and who monitored the media consumption of their kids, ended up having a greater sense of empowerment. However, because today's devices are portable, and more and more people carry the Internet with them everywhere they go, it's impossible for parents to monitor media consumption.

Remember when the greatest fear for parents was their kids "talking" to strangers or pedophiles? Only a few years ago, families had rules requiring teens to use the Internet only in open places in the home, such as the kitchen. Parents could glance over their kids' shoulders to make sure they were doing their homework, or at least using the Internet to chat with their friends. Parents were doing their jobs.

But as the Internet became mobile, parents lost their control over content. What happened to the logic? Families that were concerned enough to build "computer" desks in their kitchens were, within a few years, handing a ten-year-old a smartphone with free-for-all access to *every-thing* imaginable on the Internet and nonstop social media communication.

According to Dr. Gwenn O'Keeffe, the lead author of the new American Academy of Pediatrics social media guide-lines, "Facebook depression" is something that teachers and parents should be aware of. She says that online harassment, extensive use, and exposure to negative messages can "cause profound psychosocial outcomes," including suicide. Here's the irony: the suggestion to parents on how to deal with this very important issue is to *talk* about it. Yet we're cultivating an entire society that believes that we don't *have* to talk any-more, or who believe that posting and texting *are* the same as talking verbally. This is a mixed message we're sending. It's very confusing to our kids, and very dangerous as well.

MIXED MESSAGES

On March 10, 2011, reporter Jamie Gangel did a story on NBC's *The Today Show* about the growing use of texting. She interviewed the publisher of *Wired* magazine, who actually explained that talking and making phone calls are antiquated uses of communication in this day and age; everyone is just texting. Clive Thompson said, "When you think about it, it's a disastrously bad technology...it's dying because it deserves to die."

How this statement went unchallenged is beyond me. Think of the benefits of talking: getting things off your chest, receiving instant verbal and nonverbal cues to your thoughts and ideas, hearing the tone in someone's voice, and being able to comprehend meaning through emotions and in the way we say things. I couldn't believe that Gangel was casually joking about this. Later in the piece she sheepishly said, "Yeah, I have to admit, I don't really talk anymore, I'm doing this" as she demonstrated the now ubiquitous thumb-communication gesture.

What was profoundly ironic is that during the following hour, there was a different news piece featuring Rebbie Jackson, the oldest member of the famous musical Jackson family. She was on a tour of schools with her "Pick Up the Phone" lecture about the benefits of suicide hotlines and the importance of calling someone and *talking* if you're depressed. The story, by reporter George Lewis, featured a young woman who was saved because she called a hotline during one of her down moments. If it hadn't been for the empathetic response from the well-trained crisis counselor who gave her immediate support and listened to her, she might not have made it. As communication scholar Sandra Collins writes in her business series on listening and responding, "People who have only one person who will *listen* to them can have a more positive self-image than those who don't have anyone. In particular, empathic listening has the ability to transform lives."

In a landmark case, Rutgers University student Dharun Ravi was convicted of 15 charges, including invasion of privacy and bias intimidation (the equivalent of a hate crime) for using his webcam to spy on his roommate Tyler Clementi as he was engaged in an intimate sexual relationship. Ravi dared his Twitter followers to iChat with him to "check it out" as he turned on his webcam remotely.

What Ravi didn't realize was that Clementi was among those who were following his tweets and later learned all about Ravi's antics. Within days, Clementi posted an announcement on Facebook, writing, "I'm going to jump off the George Washington Bridge...sorry." Ravi did text an apology, but it was received 15 minutes after Tyler Clementi jumped to his death. On *CBS This Morning*, March 18, 2012, Seton Hall University law professor Mark Poyer said, "It's very bizarre that the two of them were in this small room and if they had just *talked*" to each other perhaps this tragedy might have been avoided.

In fact, during Ravi's first public interview, with *20/20*'s Chris Cuomo on March 23, 2012, Ravi explained his side of the story and clarified some media inaccuracies. Ravi admitted he learned a difficult lesson about communicating in the digital age, saying, "I wish I talked to him more, because it seemed like the only people he was talking to were people online that would never see him. I think if he had someone to talk to, really day to day life, it might have helped him." The most enlightening part of the interview was when Ravi said it was just a "normal way kids talk to each other, we're not really thinking about what if someone else reads this, how are they going to feel?" Exactly.

For all our education about creating more tolerance for one another, the ability to express your thoughts, comments, and jokes through the illusion of a protective screen allows a greater level of insensitivity to flow through the thumbs. During the interview, we discovered that Tyler Clementi was also communicating in this so-called "normal" way. His digital history of texts and tweets revealed the same insensitivity to other people's feelings.

Both students used technology to learn about one another. As Ravi found out about Clementi and texted "Fuck, he's gay," Clementi's trail of texts showed comments such as "I got an 'asian'" and "his parents definitely owned a Dunkin' Donuts." Ravi's candor seemed to underscore the growing concern by many developmental experts who are focusing their studies on an increase in narcissistic behavior for both the Millennials and the iGeneration. Ravi explained, "Looking back, I was very self-absorbed through the whole thing. It was just about what I was thinking, what I was reacting to, the whole thing."

> *According to the National Institutes of Health, 58 percent more college students scored higher on a narcissism scale in 2009 than in 1982.*

This conversation substantiates what has been happening to millions of others who were and continue to be socialized with our new tools of communication. As we communicate more and more through screen time, and less and less through (authentic) face time, we are losing the personal connection and empathy for one another. The emotional distance facilitates insensitivity and selfishness. It becomes more and more about "me" getting my thoughts out, rather than thinking of how my words, messages, and behavior affect others.

These generations — the iGeneration (the children and teens) and the "Millennials" (the young adults) — are the fastest growing population since the baby boom generation. The lesson we need to learn from tragedies brought on by increased levels of meanness and thoughtless communication, along with increasing levels of anxiety and depression, is that we need to focus a greater part of our education — not only within school, but within the home — on learning how to talk and listen to one another face-to-face. Perhaps a proven communication tool that has nurtured the human spirit for thousands and thousands of years is something to value and is worth holding onto.

In class discussions, I hear statements such as "I know I should talk to him/her in person, but I just can't seem to find the guts." Other students chime in with "Oh, I know" or show through their facial expressions that they clearly relate. When I ask my students why they don't talk face-to-face, they typically joke, "It's too scary," and everyone laughs. Or, I'll get a response with a more serious tone: "I don't want to be that vulnerable." When I say to them, "Well, you can't really fall in love and have a deep level of intimacy unless you take some risks and allow yourself to be vulnerable," I watch their faces as they realize that this is a life skill they may need to work on in order to fulfill matters of the heart.

Dr. John Cacioppo, a distinguished professor at the University of Chicago, wrote an article on the growing epidemic of loneliness. He explains that our connection to one another "is what we say we value more than anything else. In surveys to determine the factors that contribute most to human happiness, respondents consistently rate connection to friends and family — love, intimacy, social affiliation — above wealth or fame, even above physical health."

I cited his article, published in *Psychology Today,* as I explained to my students that although we spend time building a curriculum to teach the skills people need to make money and build careers, we rarely devote the time and energy to build and learn communication skills for our personal happiness. I found it pretty telling when students asked, "What is the name of the article?" and "Can you give us a handout?" The trigger word seemed to be "loneliness."

The fear of loneliness is compelling to the human psyche. We are incredibly vulnerable to the sale of any device that promises "connection." For adolescents and young adults, the idea of loneliness is usually equated with being a "loser," and there is nothing more frightening to this young population than feeling like a "loser."

In order to create fulfilling relationships, we have to be brave enough to be vulnerable. Creating social relationships is about being accepted by others individually and being accepted as part of social groups. The opposite of acceptance is rejection. What's important to understand is that it's absolutely normal to fear rejection. In fact it's actually part of our hard-wiring. As Cacioppa explains, "When we confront social rejection, the experience activates the same areas [of the brain] that light up when we are subjected to *physical* pain." So, trying to avoid being rejected is not just emotional, but biological.

The problem within our society today is that we have too many easy outs. In a study on Facebook users, Cacioppa says his research "suggests that lonely individuals tend to use social networking sites in a way that puts distance between themselves and others, whereas non-lonely people tend to use social networking sites in a way that reduces the distance."

SAFETY BEHIND THE SCREEN

"It's really becoming a culture of meanness. Safely nit picking (everyone) behind a computer. Come out in the daylight and let's have a conversation about it."
Julia Roberts, *Access Hollywood* interview, March 2012

It's called "keyboard courage." Julia Roberts is correct in her observation that today's meaner world allows us to be more judgmental of others. Many actors steer clear of negative media information that affects their spirit. They avoid reading film or theater reviews, celebrity gossip pages, or the *National Enquirer*. However, today everyone who uses social media is vulnerable to what I call "sucker punch" communication.

People participate in social media sites for the promised connections and to fulfill their human need for communing with others. Yet, for no apparent reason, they can be subjected to hurtful, insulting, sometimes extraordinarily cruel and thoughtless words or defaming pictures because of someone else's personal insecurities, random judgments, or mean spirit. This personal violation can be very destructive.

There are too many stories of kids and young adults having "friends" Photoshop images on their Facebook pages "as a joke" or to be mean. There are also too many stories of false accusations that defame someone's reputation, or rumors that spiral out of control. The same defamatory comments we seem to tolerate in the social media era might have been admissible as a libel lawsuit only a few years ago. Right now, there are no established laws that cover the evolving elements of cyber activity or even laws that can clearly identify some behavior as criminal. Meanwhile, much of this keyboard-courage communication remains as destructive as any physical punch, sometimes more.

In his book *Nonviolent Communication: A Language of Compassion,* Dr. Marshall Rosenberg explains that "judgments of others are alienated expressions of our own unmet needs." This is not a call to condemn those who act out in a mean spirit or through thoughtless communication. We need to understand that those people also have needs that are not being met. We talk about the "bullying" epidemic and focus on "punishing" the bullies. However, if they have not been taught compassion or empathy, how can they *feel* it toward others?

A news story described a 12-year-old Rhode Island girl who was beaten up by her "friends" because she said a boy was cute. She had previously survived nine operations to deal with water on the brain, yet was kicked in the head and beaten up by four girls from school. The incident was even caught on tape. A man across the street was more interested in capturing the image to post on YouTube and turning the camera on himself for added commentary than in breaking up the fight.

The four 12- and 13-year-olds were arrested. In a news report, the mother of one of the assailants expressed remorse for what her daughter did and said, "My daughter needs help. She's done this too many times." What does it say about our humanity when someone can watch a fight involving young girls and be more concerned about posting the video rather than helping to save a life?

Thankfully, the victim survived. If she had died from one wrong kick to the head, this would have been a national story, and the man might have been arrested for failing to stop a fight or for not calling the police.

How insensitive have we become? Have the images become so common that we can't even feel that each punch or kick actually causes pain? The four assailants will also forever be branded "bullies." The documented image that was posted on YouTube will have captured the worst moment of their adolescence. It will shape them and their images of themselves, just as it will shape their victim. She will never be able to delete that horrific moment of her life — once something has been posted on the Internet, it is always somewhere out there. Even if YouTube removes it, you still know it can show up in your life when you least expect it. Even if the incident is eventually resolved, and all the girls get therapy and mature and learn and grow, it will always be floating around...somewhere. Not exactly a peaceful way to live.

As we have seen with the Ravi/Clementi case and other tragic stories, online drama is a part of daily life for many people, and it is having a negative impact on individuals and families. Being embarrassed in front of a few people is bad enough. However, 21st-century technology has amplified the level of public humiliation and embarrassment, broadcasting these incidents to a much wider audience. Even our most evolved and confident adults would find these incidents difficult to deal with. For adolescents, who can be more emotionally fragile during this time in their development, these situations can be particularly horrifying and even deadly.

For all the benefits of modern communication technology, the downside is that it's stripping away the number of personal interactions and experiences our young people need in order to build a sense of personal accountability, emotional intelligence, empathy, and compassion. How are today's young people going to become mature adults capable of trusting and having intimate relationships without the experiences of learning and building the skills they need?

Every time we face a screen instead of a person, we lose an opportunity to practice the interpersonal communication we need in order to expand our emotional intelligence. We can't learn how to read body language, establish a bond, receive a message intuitively, create memories, or gain a deeper level of human connection through a text. Different studies report that from 60 to 90 percent of the messages we send and receive in face-to-face communication are nonverbal. There is no substitute through technology.

When you look up the word "screen," the first word that comes up is "separate." Synonyms include "partition," "protection," "filter," "concealment," and "hide." The word "monitor" has also been added as part of our contemporary vernacular. In the early 1900s, screens were used to project motion picture films and also to separate our reality from the illusions of Hollywood. In the 1950s, a smaller screen entered our homes.

When the 60s brought us graphic images of the Vietnam War on the evening news, television images in our living rooms fueled protests and public outrage. But by the time we got to the 80s, with cable offering 24/7 TV content, our televisions never rested, and neither did we. When we entered the 90s, the focus shifted a bit from content to the amount of time children were spending in front of the television and the use of television as a babysitter. Hundreds of studies *concluded* that parents should limit the amount of "screen" time for kids.

The explosion of the video game industry offered interactive screen-time entertainment. Video games were later attacked for contributing to childhood obesity, as kids spent hypnotic hours exercising their hand dexterity and little else. Concerns about anti-social behavior, game addiction, and overstimulation had pediatricians issuing warnings and suggesting limits on use. And, after all that, we ushered in the home computer age, with all the excitement reminiscent of the 50s television era. The portability factor meant that a child could now bring the once-discouraged television screen everywhere. Out went all the statistics and recommendations from pediatricians, in exchange for the relief of knowing that if their children had enough games, or a portable DVD player, then parents didn't have to worry about a cranky child on a long road trip.

So the question is, what happened to all that indisputable research and wisdom that empirically concluded that children, teens, and people in general need less screen time and more personal human interaction on a daily basis? Why is it that now, in the digital age, we accept the ubiquitous face-to-screen behavior blindly and without question? Why is this socially acceptable now? This makes no logical sense at all. We are still humans, with the same human needs.

Regardless of the research and logic, the fact is that if you were born in the late 80s or in the 90s, you've been socialized with a screen in front of your face. Young adults today are the "screenagers" of the 90s. Over the years, we have seen studies showing that increased screen time may actually hinder language and social development. There are plenty of documentaries showing the effects of too much gaming and its potential addictive nature. Do we need any new studies when we haven't paid attention to the old ones?

> "Sanity is not statistical."
> — George Orwell

If we know the facts and we choose to ignore them, are we in fact "celling our souls" and leaving ourselves to deal with the consequences? Think about people who continue to smoke. Devoted smokers say things like, "My grandmother smoked until she was 99 and never got cancer," to justify their own bad habit. It will take a couple of decades of research to undeniably prove the link between increased screen-time communication during developmental years and its negative effect on social skills and intimacy in adulthood. However, common sense may need to be the catalyst for addressing the issue of why so many young people are feeling a sense of disconnection.

EMOTION OUTWEIGHS LOGIC

Intellectually, the 'tweens and 20-somethings *know* they need to develop face-to-face and verbal communication skills. Intellectually, they know and can list all the reasons why they should be talking instead of texting. They understand that you "don't get the whole story, can't read body language, and can't hear the emotion in someone's voice."

What I've come to learn is that their fear makes them cave into texting rather than confronting the conflict or the potential vulnerability they might be subject to within an emotion-bearing conversation. As an NYU student said in the *Today Show* piece on the declining use of phone calls, texting "takes away the awkwardness of the actual interaction on the phone."

Teenagers send and receive an average of 3,276 texts per month, 24 hours per day.
Neilson Company Statistic for last quarter of 2010

If this generation is constantly avoiding "awkward" conversations with friends, how are they going to build the social skills and confidence to work with strangers in a professional setting? Learning to overcome the fear is what builds the confidence and communication skills so many career and social environments demand.

One of my students, a fashion retail major, couldn't wait to tell me of her proud communication accomplishment. "OK, so, here's what happened. So, when I got to work, I saw that one of the women that I work with had her name on this list which said that she was supposed to get the commission of this big (account) sale that was actually mine! I was freaking out, literally, my heart beating trying to figure out how to handle this. I really wanted to text her to say, "Why is your name next to this?" But then, thinking of everything we've been learning in this class, I knew that there was nothing that I could write in a text that would 'sound' right to the 'receiver' of that message."

We were all laughing a bit because the way she was saying what she wanted to text sounded so sweet, with this "Gosh, golly, gee, I was just wondering" sort of tone, but we all knew, that her "tone" would never translate into a text, and she knew it as well. "So, I got up the nerve and I called her, I was so nervous because she was pregnant and I didn't want to upset her, but when I said something like 'I'm not sure if you knew…(very sweet and sincerely spoken), that that was my sale…' and she just (responded) said, 'Oh my God, I'm so sorry…I must have done that accidently, I'm just not thinking these days, be sure to change it so your name is there.' I couldn't believe how easy that was! I can't believe how nervous I was, but I felt so much better after just clearing it up!"

When I ran into this student at her portfolio show where she was presenting her work in a lovely and very polished and professional way, we laughed about that incident, and she reaffirmed that that one little lesson had increased her confidence.

As students hear stories like these coming from their peers, they relate to the feelings of fear, saying things like "I won't even call for pizza now that you can order online." They know that good communication skills are still needed, no matter how great technology is. Inevitably, during some of these discussions on why we feel the way we feel, the question "What about Skype" comes up. "That's when you can use technology to get face time, right?" As if to say, maybe I don't ever have to come out of my room.

Yes, Skype can be very effective for some interpersonal communication. However, it's important to keep in mind that any use of a "screen" still separates and filters to a certain degree. For some people, there is still a sense of being "on" for the camera. Like all new technology, Skype can be an incredible communication tool for the right situation. But it's still not a replacement for authentic human connections when we have the opportunity for them.

Here's why it is important to become a more discerning user of media. When we gain a greater understanding of our human needs and then match those needs to the right communication experience or tool, we can incorporate technology into our world in a more balanced way. Sometimes the right communication experience will not involve anything other than our own human apps, and that's what can be scary, especially when we have become so dependent on our devices that they are an extension of us.

Again, the problem isn't the technology itself; the problem is the misconception that new technology is a substitute for authentic connection. For military men and woman overseas, Skype can be a wonderful tool to keep families together and be able to watch children grow. When grandparents live too far away to see their grandchildren, or parents need to *see* their kids away at college looking good and healthy, Skype can be an incredible contribution to the world of communication.

Skype sleeping? I'm not so sure. This, as explained by many students, involves falling asleep with your laptop up and the camera facing you while you sleep. Your "partner" also has his or her laptop up while they're sleeping. As one student explained, "That way, if you wake up in the middle of the night, you can look over and see that the other person is there, and you feel better." Perhaps this is a contemporary intimacy builder that is too new to evaluate as anything other than an alternative way to connect.

The comments from the class ranged from a student whose husband was in the military and appreciated the ability to feel closer, to other students who would "Skype sleep" with a friend who lives a few miles away, to others who found "Skype sleeping" a bit much and made comments like "I don't want anyone watching me drool in my sleep" or "That's just creepy."

FEAR FUELS COMPULSION

The fear of being alone for any length of time, or the fear of not being able to connect with someone when you want to know something or feel reassured, or the fear of something showing up on your "wall" that might embarrass you, has contributed to the compulsiveness of always needing to check. Listen to the daily internal dialogue you're having with yourself. Listen to the language. We're compelled to constantly check because we're asking ourselves "Does somebody need me?" So, follow the logic. If someone "needs" you, you feel wanted, and that feels good. When you check and nobody "needs" you, you feel unwanted, and that feels bad. Research shows that this constant checking, this looking for a quick hit of dopamine (the brain chemical that makes us feel good), is behavior as compulsive as a gambler being unable to walk away from a slot machine.

THE INFORMATION AGE

In the past 20 years, personal computers have become part of our home life, work life, education system, and political landscape. They have created globalized connections that unite cultures and countries. We have gone from a gigantic $1,500 wireless phone, which needed a luggage cart to be moved from place to place, to a tiny combination of home computer and wireless phone that is totally "free" as long as you pay a monthly service fee. We have transformed and revolutionized the way our world works and connects. Amazing.

"It's an invention's intellectual ethic that has the most profound effect on us. The intellectual ethic is the message that a medium or other tool transmits into the minds and culture of its users."
—Nicholas Carr, *The Shallows*

From Thomas Edison to Steve Jobs, innovative thinkers have tapped into their brilliance because they can brainstorm without any limits. The creative process, whether it's in the arts or sciences, cannot be stifled. To the determined inventor, obstacles are mere inconveniences.

Traditionally, technophiles focus on the never-before-seen or never-before-even-imagined aspects of innovations. They enjoy meeting the challenge of bringing science fiction to life and pleasing themselves with the emotional gratification of "Look what I can do!" As Nicholas Carr writes in his book *The Shallows*, "The intellectual ethic of a technology is rarely recognized by its inventors. They are usually so intent on solving a particular problem or untangling some thorny scientific or engineering dilemma, that they don't see the broader implications of their work. The users of the technology are also usually oblivious to its ethic."

Over the years, inventors of mechanically engineered pieces of communication technology have reveled in the kudos of their peers and have been monetarily rewarded for their world-changing inventions. As computers have become faster and faster and smaller and smaller, the world has applauded with fascination and "How'd you do that?" curiosity. Meanwhile, those in the human sciences could do little but watch and observe.

Social scientists, psychologists, media scholars, sociologists, and anthropologists do what they do. They watch and observe with cautious curiosity, jotting down notes, observing patterns of behavior, questioning and listening, making more notes, and discussing their thoughts with peers and other professionals. They line up questions for professional studies, because theories and observations alone do not hold any weight in this day and age.

Maybe Aristotle could make an observation about human behavior and have it last for centuries as a strong truth. Today, unless the philosopher could *prove* it or had reams and reams of corroborating data, no one would believe him. And even then, we tend to believe only what we want to believe.

THE TRUTH REVEALED

It's hard to ignore the expressions on the faces of young people when we actually start to sit down and have an open and honest discussion about how they feel about life in the digital world. In these group discussions and one-on-one conversations, I've heard some compelling stories about the confusion and byproducts caused by our communication technology. My inner social scientist has been on overload, watching and observing. As I have expanded my teaching into interpersonal communication studies, I've had to move into the world of those being affected by technological changes so I could address the issues as seen through their eyes.

"The high-minded man must care more for the truth than
for what people think."
— Aristotle

I observed, listened, hugged, helped with problem solving, experimented, read, researched, and most importantly, learned from beautiful young minds. I asked about changes in their personal lives. Are they being heard, do they feel understood, what is stressing them out, what areas are they struggling with, how are they using technology in their everyday lives, what is upsetting them, how do they feel about how society uses technology?

I came to understand that despite the increasing use of technology in their lives, it didn't seem to be making their lives better, easier, more enriched, or happier. In class, we discussed the confusion of trying to figure things out while still coming across as if you were "cool."

One student said, "Yeah, we were like 12 when we had flip phones, and I remember someone texting me something with just letters and a number...cul8r...I couldn't for the life of me figure out what the heck that meant! I was trying all day to figure it out."

Regardless of what anyone said to him all day or what he was learning in school, he was mentally trying to solve the mystery. "See you later." So forget about trying to figure out life in high school. Now you have to figure out a whole new language and deal with the peer pressure of not being cool if you don't speak it! One student said, "But at least back then you just left it in your locker and you didn't have to respond all day. Now, we're checking our phones every two seconds!" A second student replied, "Yeah, but don't middle school and high school students still have to keep them in their lockers...so, they sorta still can go through the day without their phones."

I thought the same thing until a 14-year-old middle school student set me straight. In 2011, he said, "UGGs were made for texting." He went on to explain that girls keep their phones in their high UGG boots, bend down to "adjust" their "socks," and send text messages to each other all day long. Today, most high schools have just given up policing cell phone use. Students are texting all day long with each other throughout their school day. As soon as they leave the classroom, there is a universal element of emotional relief as kids can finally check their phones for possible earth-shattering news. If anticipating what they might find on social media is weighing heavy on their minds during each class, then how much learning is going on? We all have to battle a certain level of external noise, but the level of distractions that we have to battle on a daily basis in the digital age is astronomical.

According to the technology research company *text plus*, 66% of *parents* will text their kids in school, even when kids are not supposed to have their phones on them. The nonstop communication, and more importantly, the expectation and pressure to keep up and respond immediately, is causing stress and anxiety. Parents think that "if it's me, it's OK," but forget that *it's the conditioning to check* that is creating the obsessive behavior. Our culture is creating the pressure and unrealistic expectations of having to know everything about everyone all the time.

Have we stopped to think about why we need to know so much and what this need is doing to us? In addition to traditional news and information, the constant stream of "personal" information about everyone we've "friended" is too much. We can't possibly care about so many people and what is going on in their lives. Trying to figure out who we need to care about, and whose information we can filter out, is exhausting and mentally draining.

> "The great gift of human beings is that we have the power of empathy."
> — Meryl Streep

We're now seeing data that reveals what social scientists, psychologists, teachers, and others have been witnessing and feeling in our guts. The University of Michigan did a study involving over 14,000 college students combining 72 different studies on student attitudes from 1979 to 2009. The research showed that there has been a dramatic decline in the way that these young people *feel* about other people. It shows that today's generation of young adults are about 40% *less* empathic than those of the 1980s and 1990s.

This study underscores the *disconnect* that today's kids have been feeling. One of the study items, which asked whether students valued "putting oneself in the place of others or to try to understand their feelings," showed a low score. In the U-M news release of the study, researcher Sara Konrath explains that "compared to 30 years ago, the average American now is exposed to three times as much non-work-related information. In terms of media content, this generation of college students grew up with video games, and a growing body of research, including work done by my colleagues at Michigan, is establishing that exposure to violent media numbs people to the pain of others." To see such a drastic shift in values in such a short period of time is concerning.

As a society, it is easy for us to turn a blind eye to the warnings about things that might not be good for us. We're receiving so much pleasure from theses "bad things" that we find it easy to justify our behavior. We over-indulge. We supersize our food, drinks, and alcohol. And we're doing the same with technology. When these indulgences bring us so much pleasure, we find it easy to justify our behavior. Some people are finally starting to recognize the dangerously powerful pull of our digital world. I asked a friend of mine a few years ago if she was on Facebook. She replied, "With my addictive personality, I won't go near it." I found it interesting that she recognized the addictive quality of Facebook as soon as it became mainstream. Here is an adult who has learned enough about herself to be able to make that choice.

Yet, because social media doesn't seem to be "consumable," we don't believe that it can be harmful. It's the "That's just what we do today, I guess" attitude. Graduate student Edward O'Brien, who was also on the University of Michigan research team, explains the effect of social media on the decreasing level of empathy: "The ease of having 'friends' online might make people more likely to just tune out when they don't feel like responding to others' problems, a behavior that could carry over offline."

This is a problem. It's a problem because we cannot exist without one another. And the quality of our interactions is going to dictate the success of our society. In 2005, best-selling author Daniel Pink released the book *A Whole New Mind: Why Right-Brainers Will Rule The Future.* Pink dedicated an entire chapter to the importance of empathy, saying, "It is much more than a vocational skill necessary for surviving twenty-first century labor markets. It's an ethic for living. It's a means of understanding other human beings...a universal language that connects us beyond country or culture. Empathy makes us human. Empathy brings joy...empathy is an essential part of living a life of meaning."

Every time we show the highly acclaimed PBS documentary *Growing Up On Line* in class, there is one particular scene that generates the "Oh, that's so sad" response and other emotional and cringing expressions. Filmmaker Rachel Dretzin takes us into the home of a typical New Jersey family. Everyone is isolated in their own space of the house, engaged in some computer communication or video game. A young boy, maybe eight years old, is playing a game with animated characters. A little character pops up and prompts the young boy to click on something, and the boy says, in the sweetest little voice "Oh, he wants to be my friend." Many students in the class sigh, "Ohhh, that's so sad." I ask my students why they react this way, and their collective view is that he just seems "so lonely."

The other scene that gets a big response is when one middle school-age girl is explaining social media and how many friends she has (in the hundreds), and then says "But you can really only have like 50 *best* friends." My college-age students cry "Oh my God" because the girl doesn't understand what a best friend is. But, the other middle school-age girls in the documentary are not at all fazed by the "50 best friends" remark, and judging by the looks on their faces, seem to be thinking, "Yeah, that seems about right." Perhaps a reexamination of the meaning of "friend" is appropriate at this stage of the digital game?

The University of Michigan study produced some tangible data to explain the feelings and attitudes of young adults today. And it's no wonder that this group has lost some empathy — they've been the test subjects of what is, in actuality, a global social experiment. It's easy for adults to say, "What are they, stupid? Don't they know that everything you put up online goes out to everyone!"

No. They are not stupid. They are the first generation of people who have had to learn how to socialize and develop their self-identities and friendships through technology rather than through the slower, more natural process of human interactions. We have never done it this way before, and this generation has virtually been the lab rats.

Adolescence is confusing enough, and yet this group had to figure out a new, uncharted way of building friendships, ending friendships, being in touch, not being in touch. How much privacy do I need? If I don't have an online image, will I be left out? What image do I want to create? Who do I want to be? Create an appropriate image, wait to be judged, change the image, be judged again, and ignore hurtful words from kids protected by the "only kidding" mantra. I believe in the philosophy that my former dean had framed in her office: "Once a truth is known it cannot be ignored, only denied."

It's easy for us to say, "Back in my day, we flitted around without a care in the world," and remember the joys of having a free spirit. This generation never had that luxury. They were born into a media-saturated environment, targeted as consumers for an over-commercialized culture. As with all generations before, we just assumed they'd adapt to the environment unscathed. But, as we're seeing, they aren't.

When we see that an entire generation has lost an important part of what makes us human, it's time to reevaluate our priorities. Continued research is imperative in order to substantiate a call to action. In the meantime, empathetic group conversations in classrooms and one-on-one, face-to-face, full-attention dialogue at home and between one another can teach empathetic communication, perhaps relieve some stress, build intimacy and trust, and even reveal other areas where technology has inadvertently affected aspects of the human experience.

It's pretty normal to be enamored with something that provides so much pleasure. If you've ever been in love, you remember that in the beginning, you just don't want to know anything negative. You can have all your friends telling you why he isn't good for you, or how she ruined the last guy she was with, and you will simply justify your relationship. That's why the NYU student on the *Today Show* story on texting could say "I lovvvve my BlackBerry." We can love things that aren't necessarily good for us.

> *In 1964, The United States Surgeon General's office releases a new report that clearly and definitively links smoking cigarettes with causing cancer. Previously, big tobacco companies advertised and sold their damaging product as something for the general public to enjoy.*

When my nieces and nephew were little kids and had their feelings hurt, sometimes just from having a toy taken away from them by another child, they would cry and say "I feel bad" as the tears rolled down their cheeks. I remember that my sister would sweetly hold them, and then put her hand on her heart and rub it a little. With her thumb and forefinger, she would delicately remove an imaginary section from the middle of her chest and hand it over, saying, "I'm so sorry you're feeling so sad, and here's a little piece of my heart to make you feel better."

She would then place the imaginary piece on the heart of the crying child where they would both pat it in a bit, and she would say, "I'm sharing this little piece of my heart to help heal that little hurt piece of your heart." The tears would slowly subside, as the frown turned into a gentle smile. It was a parental routine. When I had my own child, I was a big copycat and did the same thing.

The philosophy I share with my students in our personal communication studies is that "The *only* thing to do with a feeling is to honor it." When it comes to human emotions, we have to value feelings and act on them. We don't say to a little child who is upset, "Well, do you have any proof, perhaps some stats to show me why you're upset?" So when students and young people are saying that the demands of 21st-century 24/7 communication are making them feel stressed out and anxious, why are we ignoring them? It may be years before science can substantiate their feelings with overwhelming statistics, but by then the damage will be done. All I know is what I've heard over these past several years, as class after class and student after student have told me the same things over and over.

"I'm so addicted...it's compulsive...I don't even know I'm doing it...I freak out if I don't have my phone...I said something so stupid...I drunk texted...I feel ignored... nobody listens to me...I feel like I'm not living my own life...I'm obsessed with other people's lives instead of my own...I can't seem to stop following ...I 'said' [posted online] some really mean things I'm not very proud of...Oh my God, I'm so mortified [on posting a picture that they regret]...I feel violated [someone else posted something without permission]...she/he told everyone on Facebook...I started this whole thing on Facebook...I was just venting...it was impulsive...I didn't mean to...I can't remove it..."

As we have learned from history, there are always unforeseen consequences and ramifications associated with new inventions. Some unintended elements are positive and some are negative. We always have to weigh the risks and examine the costs in order to decide how we want to incorporate these things into our personal lives and our society as we move forward.

Chapter 8

Your Future

Individually, and as a society, we have been conditioned to obey the mediated messages that we take in almost hypnotically. We are emotionally and developmentally shaped by the media puppet masters and don't believe we can cut the strings and take charge of own lives and our own futures.

> *The Kaiser Family Foundation calculates media consumption at 7 hours and 38 minutes per day. Considering the fact that we are using media simultaneously and multi tasking, our consumption is actually more than 11 hours per day.*

Are they right? Decade after decade we have issued the statistics on our media consumption and have concluded with each new report that it's too much for any one human to deal with, yet we have done nothing to reverse the trajectory. The message that we receive from big media is designed to tap into the part of the human psyche that seeks pleasure. And we believe that easy, fast, and convenient is the model for that pleasure. But we know, contrary to what the advertising world wants us to believe, that "easy, fast and convenient" does not always translate to "better" or "fulfilling."

Do the math. If we're spending so much time interacting with our devices, there is not a lot of time left in the day to interact with our people. Many of us find that to be dangerous for humanity, but others believe that's progress.

There are two schools of thought. Many people absolutely believe we are on the right track, moving toward a world built on technological achievement, and that anyone who is not joining this path will be left out. And there are others who believe that we have gone off on a dangerous tangent in our human evolution.

THE SINGULARITY MOVEMENT

There are people who believe that without technology *augmenting* us digitally, creating a new species of enhanced humans, we may be doomed. This group also believes in creating robots with a conscience. Their truth is that their technological contributions are part of our "natural" evolution.

In February 2011, *Time* magazine's cover story was called *"2045—THE* YEAR *MAN BECOMES IMMORTAL."* Writer Lev Grossman examined the Singularity movement and reminded us that we are in fact living it right now. I know I hear it every day with comments like "My phone is an extension of me...I feel like it's a part of me...if I don't have my phone I feel incomplete...I'm totally lost without my phone..."

We have signs of dehumanization all around us. The Droid commercial uses the word *"augmentation"* and then offers the pitch line, *"This is not an upgrade to your phone, this is an upgrade to yourself."* For the Microsoft Windows phone, there are billboards all over inviting you to "meet Jessica," referring to actress Jessica Alba — who is apparently not a person anymore, she IS the phone.

Grossman's research takes into consideration the exponential growth in digital technology that has occurred over the past 30 years and explains how those in the singularity movement calculate the inevitable rise of technology over the next 30 years. For example, 30 years ago a computer took up an entire room, and now the same technology can fit on the tip of a finger. Doesn't it make sense that if this is how fast technology can change, the year 2045 sounds like a reasonable trajectory for our Cyborg world?

As Grossman reports, there are "already 30,000 patients with Parkinson's disease that have neural implants...and... more than 2,000 robots that are fighting in Afghanistan alongside human troops."

This type of technology sounds like a godsend for those suffering from the debilitating effects of Parkinson's disease, and obviously we should sacrifice some robots for our flesh-and-blood soldiers. However, is anybody overseeing a code of ethics or slippery-slope zealousness regarding the impact of these devices going mainstream? As we have said, we now know that one of our human downfalls is that we are attracted to technology that promises an "easier" life. Have we stopped to think about our human purpose if we have robots doing everything for us?

Several companies are at work every day in the field of "bioinformatics." In January 2012, IBM released their "5 in 5" report, which unveils the top five inventions they believe will become part of our world not in thirty years, but in the next five. IBM's Vice President of Innovation, Bernie Meyerson, says that just the power of your mind will control machines. In other words, you don't have to do anything or say anything. Can you imagine, people "literally thinking and having something happen as a result [of a thought]"? Technology like this is already being used so that those whose bodies are deeply impaired can still be able to communicate with others.

Other elements of these scientific advancements are coming into our everyday world. For example, how about the device that can just eliminate your email? You don't have to read it; you just look at it and kill it. As Meyerson says, "After a while it learns your habits and works for you as your assistant by eliminating stuff you never wanted anyway."

Gosh, ten years ago we were all excited about this new email system that was such an advance over regular mail, and now we can just delete it with a thought. Amazing.

Since our brains are too inefficient to remember all those passwords, technology is now being developed that will scan your fingerprint, face, voice, or eyeball, and you won't have to remember a thing. You can be scanned at the ATM and again, you *don't have to think* or anything! Just show up and say, "Hi, it's me, and I'd like my money please." As long as you're authorized by the scanner, you will receive your money. Fingerprint technology has already gone mainstream as personal identification for phones.

Oh my God, as I was writing that last line I thought of Hannibal Lecter in *Silence of the Lambs* when he took the policeman's face off in order to escape. And, I'm sure I saw a movie where someone took somebody's eyeball out in order to scan it in front of a screen to gain access to a vault or something.

Oh, but wait. Somebody should tell Bernie Meyerson that we don't need his device for ATM's, because we're already using NFC technology. Near Field Communication devices are those little square boxes with a black-and-white patterned imprint you might have seen on products or in magazines. A phone app can scan over it, and a transaction is made. NFC is a replacement for cash, credit, and debit cards.

So when all you have to do is wave your smartphone over a machine, you will never have to worry about calculating costs, counting change, taking out your wallet, or touching cash, if it even exits anymore. You will be totally removed from the emotional connection to your money. And you'll never have to teach your kids about money, since all you have to do is give them a smartphone and tell them not to "wave it all in one place."

Unfortunately, certain forms of technology enter our world and we just can't opt out of them. If the powers that be on Wall Street and in big business say that this is how we exchange goods and services, because we have the technology to do so, we are forced to be a part of the system, no matter how vulnerable it makes us feel.

The brilliant minds that have made incredible contributions to the world deserve an enormous amount of credit. What I find worrisome is what happens when the shortsighted, ego-driven ambition of achieving a technological challenge ends up devaluing our humanity and puts us on a course of idolizing our gadgets and technology rather than each other.

"I give you...LIFE"
— Gene Wilder, *Young Frankenstein*

The fact is, there are some very influential people who strongly believe that we must move forward and develop a world where humans and machine come together as one. These inventions and technological advances are created by people who are on a mission to see "if I can" and who truly believe that this is the way the world should be. Everyone has a right to his or opinion. However, there doesn't seem to be a lot of concern about the fallout or the practical consideration of how the world will function if everyone is immortal.

In Vermont, the LifeNaut Project is already collecting human consciousness, in what they're calling "mindfiles," and creating digital clones. Futurist Ray Kurzweil predicts that "by the 2030's you're not going to be able to tell a clear difference between human and machine intelligence." How this is moving at lighting speed without any ethical oversight is beyond me. Major technological changes that once took decades to affect the human experience now happen in only months. Where is the mainstream conversation about weighing the good and the bad and thinking through the long-term effects of the robotic movement on our society? Hearing a robot talk about how it "feels" and its "dreams" just seems like a big "F – U" to the human race.

The point is that as crazy as some of this stuff might sound to you now, it is happening and is being backed by millions and millions of dollars. There are really smart people who are capable of creating amazing things, who do not wish to die — ever — and who have the money and support of others who also wish to become immortal.

Ray Kurzweil is one of those spearheading the singularity movement. In addition to being a futurist whose predictions have an amazingly accurate track record, he is also a genius inventor and multimillionaire. I am a big fan of brilliance, and this man's thought process works like no other's. He has been focused on the exponential rate of information technology and believes that the pace of technological changes is only going to get faster. He is one of the founders of the Singularity University, which is supported by NASA. Kurzweil lectures all over the world. He is powerful and credible, and has influenced world leaders.

What happens when those special individuals who possess the unique combination of genius, power, money, and a desire for immortality — whether in legacy or, in this case, biology — are in a position to influence millions of people? We might want to look at history for some cautionary tales.

Kurzweil's story and vision are brilliantly brought to life in the book and documentary *The Transcendent Man*. He is praised by superstar Stevie Wonder, he is shown advising Colin Powell; he is onstage with Mick Jagger; he has actor William Shatner subscribing to his 200-pill-a-day regimen, which will assist him on his track for immortality. At 64, Kurzweil just has to live long enough to take advantage of the technology he needs to live... forever.

However, the one theme that is constant through the film and book, and through Kurzweil's own words, is his relationship with his father and how he plans to bring his father back from the dead with the technology that he's working on. Some might find this quite disturbing and, with all his genius, might just put him on the megalomaniac spectrum. Kurzweil talks about having the God-like power to be able to bring back life from the dead with such clear certainty and in such a calm, matter-of-fact way that it is convincingly eerie. Throughout the movie, he talks about the impact that his father's death had on him and how he plans to correct that, and because of his enormous genius, he trusts that he can. Again, repeating the mantra, even if we can, does it mean we should?

Back when animal cloning was a hot news topic, I remember many religious leaders, ethics scholars, and political figures debating the moral issues and long-term ramifications of technology that could in fact lead to human cloning. Stem cell research continues to spark very public debates between medical technology and moral guidelines.

Here we are talking about a world where the trajectory of man united with machines is not only totally plausible, but according to some, actually quite inevitable. If we consider how we feel about our devices today, and how the public mindlessly incorporates the latest and greatest gadgets, are we just jumping on a runaway train? The pattern continues to be that although we talk about the important elements of the human experience, and how important love and relationships are, the instant a new piece of amazing technology shows up, we lose all sight of our values.

BOLDLY GOING

As the Internet was becoming more and more mainstream, its unknown uses were ripe for all kinds of experimentation. Without any restrictions, every single person could go online and become a broadcaster, with instant mass distribution of any thought, idea, creative project, lies, propaganda, art, or anything one person considers to be art.

Humans are multifaceted. Because we need to belong, need attention, recognition, validation, love, and affection — we are vulnerable to any offer of getting those things as easy and as fast as possible. We are taught that fame will get us noticed, and perhaps then we will get more love. The alluring pull of fame, as I mentioned earlier, is the feeling that we will leave our mark on the world and gain a sense of immortality. Each one of us falls somewhere on the huge spectrum of attention needs, but as humans, we are wired to need recognition from others.

Before YouTube allowed everyone on the planet to be a TV, music, or movie star, a site called Pseudo.com, created by Internet pioneer Josh Harris, gave everyone full access to broadcast on the Internet. Harris, another major supporter of the Singularity Movement, believes we should all be living through the Internet and that every single one of us should be a "reality star."

"One day we're going to wake up and all be servants."
— Josh Harris

Harris began a major social science experiment in the 90s. The climax was a project involving 100 people who would live every single aspect of their lives in front of cameras. This experiment took place in a totally wired New York

City underground bunker-style hotel, where the volunteers lived in "pods" surrounded by cameras. Harris watched the drama and sex and unbridled emotions of his human lab rats through the TV control room.

The lack of privacy took a toll on the participants within the first few days of the 30-day experiment. Without having a single minute to even go to the bathroom privately, the participants — men, women and children — literally began to go mad. As authorities closed down the experiment, defining it as a threatening cult-like group, Harris was determined to pursue his vision. This time, he turned the cameras on himself. Harris installed cameras everywhere in his NYC loft for a live 24/7 Internet broadcast of his own personal life, including his new girlfriend. There was no editing or production. Any moment of the day, people could log on and watch them sleeping, having sex, or having a fight, and could write comments.

It didn't take very long for Harris to have a mental breakdown as the public judgments, cruel comments from his viewers, and destruction of his relationship forced him to seek solitude and a reevaluation of life. The entire story is captured in Ondi Timoner's 2009 documentary called *We Live In Public.*

This dynamic and cautionary story has basically been ignored. There's even one scene in Harris's original social experiment where he turns to the camera and explains that his volunteers should enjoy the attention, that's "free except [for] the video we capture of you...that we own." I couldn't help making the Facebook comparison; on Facebook, you put yourself out there, vulnerable to judgment and drama, and have to relinquish all rights to everything you do, say, and post, because by clicking "I agree" to the terms and conditions, you are relinquishing all rights of ownership to your personal images, thoughts, and words.

Harris's self-imposed hiatus from public view was short-lived. He is back with a new online television network called Net Band Command. The network is described as being similar to the movie *The Truman Show,* but Harris's version "encourages people to compete against each other." Harris believes everyone should have their homes wired and live life in front of the camera. And why not? There certainly seems to be a market for our voyeuristic obsession and living vicariously through the lives of others. How different is this than scrolling through our TV channels to stumble across one of the many *The Real Housewives*, of wherever series; *Jersey Shores'* Snooki, now changing diapers; or *The Kardashians,* who have built a mega million-dollar empire "just being us," as "Kardashian Mom" Kris Jenner explained.

During an interview with Oprah, Jenner said that the eclectic personalities displayed on *The Osbournes* were the inspiration for the *Keeping Up with the Kardashians* reality show. She felt that her family is so intriguing that the world would want to watch them. Nothing could have underscored the narcissistic cultural shift more than that interview. With every family member interviewed, it was "I feel, I want, I, I, I, I, me, me, me, ..." As Larry Rosen explains in his book *iDisorder,* "Media starts with *m e.*"

Ray Kurzweil and Josh Harris have some characteristics in common. Both men share a strong desire for parental validation; Kurzweil wants to show he is a great and powerful superhuman, able to bring his father back to life, and Harris actually refers to himself as "OZ," as in the great and powerful. The need for attention can be a dominating force for some people. "The way I grew up, people were legitimized by having the camera turned on them...if you made it on Johnny Carson....it was the mark of 'making it,'" Harris explained.

What concerns me is that these are people with a "puppet master" mentality, who actually have a ton of money, supporters, followers, and influence over a vulnerable society. As Harris explained during a 1999 *60 Minutes* interview, "We are in the business of programming people's lives."

We continue to be OK with this: the attention trade-off must be worth the risk. As filmmaker Ondi Timoner explains, "Everything that Harris predicted back in 1999 is happening today." We innocently surfed and posted and Googled away, not really understanding that every keystroke we have made over the past 20 years remains a documented piece of Internet history. We provided a virtual treasure trove of our personal information and data for the technically savvy to do with whatever they want.

Growing up online today can be a restriction on our free spirit. Maybe *we* didn't know the intricate workings or hidden consequences of technology when we blindly dove in, but there are people who do and who are making different personal choices, because they know better.

THE NEXT GENERATION

There is a strong understanding that behavior is the most accurate form of communication. Or, as the old saying goes, "actions speak louder than words." So, when we want to comprehend meaning, we need to look at the behavior.

What does it say when in Silicon Valley, the home of high tech, there are quite a few schools that are totally tech-free in their education philosophy, and that these are where high-tech executives and developers send their children to school?

According to an October 2011 *New York Times* article, the Waldorf School of the Peninsula boasts an old-world philosophy about technology and education. Their belief, which they've been practicing for over 100 years, is that it's important to create a teaching environment that promotes a love of learning. They focus on more physical activity and creativity, and whole-heartedly believe that "computers inhibit creative thinking, movement, human interaction and attention spans." The school administrators and faculty also don't believe in technology or computer use in the home. Google communication executive Alan Eagle says, "I fundamentally reject the notion you need technology aids in grammar school," and reports that his daughter, in fifth grade at the time of the report, does not know how to use Google.

Why then do those who make millions of dollars creating technological devices and who have, in turn, cultivated a global demand for information technology, choose to send their own children to schools with strong **anti**-technology philosophies? Isn't it a red flag along the lines of someone who wouldn't eat the food at their own restaurant? A bit suspicious, right?

The high-tech career parents at Google, Microsoft and Intel featured in the article do not see any contradiction in their actions. They believe that technology has a place in society, but as one CEO explains, "what's the rush" in learning how to use Google or any other computer skills, as these are easy skills to pick up when you're older. Meaning that the developmental years are the important times to develop those authentic problem solving skills and people skills that apparently are vital to our lives. Exactly! However, that's not the message that's getting to the public on any level.

Contrast this with the fact that, as I mentioned earlier, the *PBS* parent's website suggests that the age for an iPad is three. According to their expert, Dr. Carolyn Jaynes, "Many children are active media users and can benefit from electronic media with educational content."

I should point out that Jaynes designs games for Leapfrog, which is marketed as an "educational toy," so there may be a conflict of interest in using her as an authority. The PBS site on kids' digital devices goes on to report that Jeannie Galindo, a supervisor of instructional technology, says, "In a supervised environment, children as young as four or five are able to engage in learning activities using smartphones and tablets of all kinds." That can be true. However, we have to be honest about how these interactive devices are being used. If parents are using them as *a small part* of an *overall* interpersonal interaction, they may very well be beneficial. But the reality is that for many children, these devices are *substituting* for personal interaction.

There are different philosophies about how we should be educating our future generations. Some educators believe that our personal development through human interaction should come first. Others believe that technology should be the foundation of the classroom and that we have to constantly teach in a way that stimulates the mind in order to have kids be *able* to pay attention. This is, after all, the generation who grew up in front of video games. There is evidence showing that the 21st-century brain that grew up on technical stimulation requires a jumping-around type of thinking. The linear thinking mind that was cultivated in earlier centuries has become obsolete, so we must adapt our teaching to meet those changes.

Try This

Ask your friends and family, "If we have the talent and the genius to create super humans with super brains, should we? Is this playing God? If we can create machines that can think for us, should we? What might be some of the unintended consequences of such a world? How do you see your future?

When we have debated these questions in class, we always come back to a *feeling*. "It just doesn't feel right," "It's creepy," "It's like we're being used," "This is totally Orwell's *1984* Big Brother world," "Oh my God, this is the turning point in *The Terminator*." In spite of all our technology, we always seem to believe in our Hollywood endings. We need that one incredible human, with the authentic human apps — courage, character, love, loyalty, determination, desire, and personal strength — to save the day.

Chapter 9

Embrace Authenticity

If the Singularity "man/machine" vision isn't what you had in mind, the good news is that we're starting to see evidence of a digital backlash. You can see the signs in our media. For example, before corporations invest millions of dollars in an ad campaign, they want to make sure they develop a campaign that people will relate to; they take the time to interview their target demographics in focus groups and surveys. It seems as though advertising professionals must be hearing a lot of "I'm tired of talking to a robot" comments, as evidenced by recent banking commercials.

Earlier I mentioned Chase Sapphire Blue: *"Hello...Oh, I'm talking to a real person?"* and Ally Bank: *"If you're not talking to a real person..."* Now we're seeing more and more companies responding to people's desire to authentically connect with other people. Here are some other examples that are part of this backlash:

- Harvard Pilgrim Health Care: "People do amazing things when they work together."

- TD Bank: "It's time to bank human again."

- Wells Fargo: "The power of a conversation"

Many corporations can support their message with policy changes that reflect their values. However, for our digital devices, there is a greater challenge. Ad agencies all over are now busy creating campaigns selling the "human" experience as a benefit of their products. Remember, the "emotional sell" has been a proven strategy.

- Skype: "It's time to talk human again"

- Apple: "This is it. This is what matters. The experience of a *person*."

The problem with Apple's campaign is that if you apply one of the foremost principles of communication to this ad — that the most accurate form of communication is behavior — what you'll see is that the behavior of the actors in the commercial is the exact opposite of the campaign slogan. Nobody is putting down their device to look into the eyes of another person, or focusing their attention on the people they're with. All of them are still turning their attention away from each other and onto their devices. Apple can say that they believe the experience of a person is what matters in life; however, the behavior speaks volumes. It says, "If you want to feel loved, buy this product."

BE HUMAN

President Obama is considered our first social media president and is rarely without his BlackBerry. However, it was a purely human moment that captured the world's attention and garnered some of the most extensive media coverage of the inauguration.

As the newly sworn-in President was leaving the inaugural stage, he stopped for a few moments and turned to look out over the sea of humanity waving their flags. "I just want to take it all in" he was heard saying, as the Secret Service was caught off guard with the pause in their plan. The important memory that he took a minute to "store" was uniquely personal and emotionally fulfilling. *That* can never be "shared." It was refreshing to see how "embracing a moment" was modeled, and more importantly, valued. Perhaps we are embarking on an alternative to the Singularity types who believe in the inevitable "chip-in-our-heads" trajectory. Maybe the "peace and love" generation were on to something.

> "This is the dawning of the Age of Aquarius."
> — from the musical *Hair*

The musical *Hair* was controversial for the 60s and 70s for its anti-establishment message and for disrespecting the American flag, not to mention the shock value of long-haired actors stripping off their costumes in front of a live audience. For me, however, it was just cool that Galt MacDermott, who wrote the music for *Hair*, lived in one of the big houses behind ours. As a little kid during the Vietnam War, I remember the grownups discussing the rebellious hippies and their talk about peace and love. We used to hear the over 40-somethings saying things like "Get a job, hippie freak." All I knew was that I wanted a pair of bell-bottoms. My father, a pretty cool NYC musician himself, surprised my sister and me one night by bringing home a pair in red for her and blue for me, making us officially cool. To this day my best friend remembers that I was the first in our school to have bell-bottoms.

> "Whoever controls the media, controls the mind."
> — Jim Morrison

More than 30 years later, Green Day's *American Idiot* hit Broadway with a similar theme. This time, the backdrop was the Gulf War, and the real enemy was the mass media and the dumbing-down of an entire generation. But now, oversaturation of messages and overconsumption of causes seem to have numbed us and pacified an entire generation, zapping our energy to rise and rebel. Clicking a few "likes" or cutting and pasting a few URL's to "check this out" is about as much "fight" as anyone has in them these days.

EMBRACE AUTHENTICITY

This *doesn't* mean that we should abandon the technology of the 21st century, or even our digital devices. This is more about *not* abandoning the core beliefs and fundamental purpose of our human experience. We need to evaluate the "ethical implications of technology for human life, social norms and values, education, work and ecological impacts," according to the *International Journal of Technoethics*. If we continue to allow technology to do everything for us, what are WE here for?

The answer is to empower each one of us, and those of the next and future generations, with a view of an evolving humanity so that our technology is working only in service to the authentic human experience. Many of us have our own ideas and philosophies about "the meaning of life," but being authentically human continues to be a common denominator in the majority of theories.

LESSONS FROM LANCE

For years, seven-time Tour de France cycling champ Lance Armstrong portrayed himself as superhuman. He was steadfast in his denial that he used any type of "enhancements" in order to achieve what seemed to be humanly impossible. Most of us, who can't seem to get to the gym on a regular basis, were put to shame by the mere thought of his physical achievements.

In January 2013, Armstrong finally admitted that he had indeed been taking performance-enhancing drugs in order to achieve his victories. Why did we feel so deceived? Obviously, because he lied, but also because these "wins" were not authentically human. ***We are rooting for greatness within the limits of our humanness.***

We simply are happier when we move toward our own authenticity. I'll take my success and my failures any time, as long as they're all mine. When we try to be the best people we can be, when we do little things by ourselves, we build moments of personal satisfaction and achievement. Think about it. If you've ever cooked an entire meal all by yourself, even if it wasn't that great, you got props and admiration from your friends. If it was good, your level of personal satisfaction went right into the self-esteem bank.

Researchers at Harvard have been studying happiness for years, and their research shows that people who work with their hands are happier than people who don't. Whether chopping vegetables or knitting a sweater, we feel a sense of personal gratification. When our devices are doing everything for us, they slowly strip away the opportunities we have to achieve those moments that make us who we are and help to build our confidence.

If you spent one day walking up and talking to people whom you would normally text or talk to on Facebook, think about how much self-confidence you would build. We've been experiencing a social inferiority complex. Our digital devices are like that super kid in high school who can do everything better than we can. We can't hate him or her for it, but we think that maybe if we hang out with that "perfect person" long enough, some of those abilities will rub off on us. I'm getting the sense that we are now realizing we are not gadgets or chips capable of completing all of life's challenges in an instant. We're feeling that perhaps we should get back to the human experience and reevaluate the things that actually make us happy and more fulfilled.

AMAZING IS NOT THE SAME AS HAPPY

Maybe we need to focus on what makes us feel better, more than on amazing pieces of technology. After more than a decade of living the digital life, we're finding that the answers to our happiness and success in life are clearly connected to the development of our authentic individual selves and to our authentic relationships with others.

Try This

Think of the happiest moments of your life. Did they involve people or things? If you reflect quietly and think about the greatest laugh you've ever had, or your proudest moment, could you get that feeling from anything other than a human experience?

_____

_____

_____

_____

The universal laws of humanity have not changed over thousands of years. The truth is that we were not prepared to be swept up in a world of 24/7 human connectivity. We were not prepared for devices that replaced our dependence on other human beings. We were not prepared for such a sharp shift in values from people to devices. We were not prepared for the level of consumerism that came with each new device and Internet platform. We have never before had any examples or modeled behavior for creating and nurturing our personal relationships _within_ a digital world. The Millennial generation was the proverbial "canary in the mineshaft." As one student said, "If we're the screwed generation, the next behind us are the doomed generation."

The high school class of 2016, the first to be totally socialized in the digital world, has been subjected to an enormous amount of potential damage. In a _Newsweek_ article, "The Kids Aren't Alright," reporter Lee Siegel writes of "the perils of parenting in the digital age." Child therapist Jamie Wasserman explains that "our kids are being socialized by each other at warp speed...they're never off social duty." At least the Millennial generation has a frame of reference for shutting down.

They can actually remember having to get off the Internet because someone had to make a phone call. They may even remember when their parents watched the "Internet clock" because they had to pay for it by the minute! The younger iGeneration doesn't know any boundaries, nor have they escaped from some of the damaging effects. MIT's Sherry Turkle confirms that "we were absolutely not paying attention...a whole generation was let down."

Those socialized in the 24/7 digital era were the first to experience an extreme communication evolution. During the time when the brain is supposed to be developing the areas of emotional intelligence, they missed some major life lessons in human interaction, human values, social skills, and personal development. According to Dr. Steven Freilich, a family psychologist practicing in Medway, Massachusetts, it's not unlike what happened to the kids who ended up smoking too much pot. "It's not so much that the marijuana was so physically damaging, it's that if they were off getting stoned, they missed the period of their lives where crucial development takes place. Then they show up in my office at 30 not being able to cope, work, or have fulfilling, intimate relationships."

THE RESULTS

The past six years of our digital socialization have resulted in a generation of young adults who may not be prepared for the real world. The "tween" who started communicating with his or her thumbs at 12 is now the 18-year-old heading into college.

In March 2013, research from the Center for Profession-al Excellence at York College of Pennsylvania received a lot of media attention for concluding, "Millennials are too imma-ture at the office." The survey of 400 human resource profes-sionals shows that young adults are "arrogant...with 54%...arriving with an air of entitlement." News reports and articles, including some in the *Business Insider* and *The Wall Street Journal,* mentioned other traits that aroused concern: lack of honesty; inattentiveness; the inability to stick with a task through completion; and using technology "inappropri-ately," such as texting co-workers instead of using email or having face-to-face conversations. In addition, Millennials continued to spend too much time on Facebook and Twitter during business hours.

HOW DO THEY NOT KNOW?

We hear that all the time, whether it's from a 40-year-old talking about a 20-year-old, or a 20-year-old talking about a 15-year-old. Because technology dictates behavior, and new social norms have been changing at such a rapid speed, there's been no time to even think of establishing rules of protocol. So how could we possibly expect an entire generation to behave in a way they were never taught? They never received a clear definition of what is appropriate and what is inappropriate behavior. Where are the rules? What are the boundaries? What is the protocol?

"The worst thing you can do is to humiliate someone."
— Oprah Winfrey, talking to Lady Gaga

Today we find young kids participating in "reckless Twitter hour," where they broadcast and document their worst weekend behavior. They may publicly mortify some-one they just "hooked up" with for their bad breath or bad kissing, or Instagram their passed-out friends or themselves at the height of their intoxication. Twelve- or thirteen-year-olds tell their parents they *need* the Internet on their phone for school and for Google, and then use the "free porn" any time, anywhere. We have accepted this behavior with the "that's just what kids do today" attitude. But this behavior is not a fashion trend. It is behavior that is negatively affecting a lot of people. We have a problem that isn't being addressed.

When you spend a little more time listening, you will hear young people say, "I hate it." They are *not* feeling good about this. One group of 15-year-olds were overheard talking about one of their friends who does not have a smartphone, referring to him as being "lucky" because he doesn't have to be subjected to all the potential hurt and drama.

The only thing to do with a feeling is honor it. That is the most fundamental and most important philosophy in the human communication process. When people tell you how they feel, they are ***always*** correct.

We have to remember that the communication skills older generations grew up with and took for granted were unfortunately devalued as we were lured into the shiny-device style of connecting. Basic skills were either not taught to our children or were not practiced ***enough.*** Now we're dealing with the universal lesson of "Sometimes we don't know what we have until we've lost it." And what we seem to have realized is that we need to get these skills back.

THE PENDULUM SWING

Are we starting to see a renewed focus on authentic communication? Big corporations such as Yahoo and Best Buy are now calling for a ban on working from home. The *Washington Post* released a portion of the Yahoo memo explaining to its employees that in order "to become the absolute best place to work, communication and collaboration will be important, so we need to be working side-by-side."

A week later, Best Buy announced a similar change in their policy as part of a month-long "conversation" about their "results only" work philosophy. These changes were greeted with an enormous amount of outrage. For young members of the work force, the old-school communication values may feel like the old bait-and-switch. They were educated with an emphasis on developing their technical skills, and now they're expected to follow a business model with traditional social skills, come out from behind a screen, face people, and interact on a daily basis?

What this decade has taught us is that all of our issues and problems can only really be resolved by authentic human connections. I mentioned Amy Poehler's plea at Harvard University to put the phones down and look for the answers in the faces of others. The challenge now is to cultivate a society that supports the value of human connections while at the same time providing the tools, a reeducation in social skills, and a universally-accepted protocol to communicate and connect in the 21st-century.

"Nothing happens if you just give in, it can't be any worse than how's it's been, so it just so happens that we just might win, so whatever happens, let's begin."
—from the musical Newsies

Chapter 10

Just Tell Me What to Do

Over the past six years I have been listening to what young people say about how they feel regarding our digitally-saturated world. Because student after student has said the same things research is now substantiating, we came up with a system that has made significant improvements in the lives of many of my students.

They have encouraged me to share their stories, our conversations, and some of the tools that have worked for them. Many have become "connection converts," encouraging their friends and family to follow their lead. The bottom line, according to Emerson College student Ben Abbene, is that "you just feel better and your relationships are so much better." The sentiment has been that "this would be so much easier if everyone did this together." You can start with your family and close friends.

These strategies would also work as a nuts-and-bolts approach for middle and high school educators who are facing the same issues but who don't have a school policy or mandate to address the problem. Schools have been a traditional cornerstone for shaping our culture by providing our children with a well-rounded education. And this education provides more than a strictly academic focus. Over the years, because of the demands of meeting academic standards, other areas of the education system have become less of a priority.

According to the Massachusetts Department of Education website, the health strand of the curriculum has not been revised since October of 1999. This is the area of education that includes social and emotional health, mental health, family life, and interpersonal relationships. Since 2000, our culture has changed in relation to the way we interact with one another. Our digitalized socialization has altered our values, yet we have never adapted the curriculum to help our children assimilate to the changing world around them! That's insane.

An important goal of our education system is to prepare kids to succeed in life both personally and professionally. But we've failed our children, which is why some of today's Millennials don't know how to behave during a job interview. According to a report in *USA Today*, "Human resource professionals say they've seen recent college grads text or take calls in interviews, dress inappropriately, use slang or overly casual language and exhibit other oddball behavior." The fact is, at this point in our culture, we haven't even had the conversation about developing a *consensus* on what is appropriate and inappropriate communication behavior.

This is usually when I hear, "It's the parent's fault." Many students rush to tell me that parents should just say No when their children demand expensive devices just to "fit in" or so that they can text nonstop, day and night. And sometimes it *is* the parent's fault. But remember, as the digital world changed our social norms and continues to influence our social behavior, it's hard for *parents* to determine what is appropriate and inappropriate communication conduct. The reality is that if every child is communicating through texting rather than talking, then that *is* the norm.

The lack of digital protocol is also an ongoing debate for professionals who have been in the work force for years. People are fed up with a workplace where staff members are multitasking, half listening, or sending texts or emails during meetings instead of having a meaningful, focused conversation.

THE CHALLENGE

There is no doubt that igniting social change is a monumental challenge. There is a philosophy that "He who controls the media controls the world." We know that media shapes us; however, the ironic thing is that, now more than ever, we the **people** have more power in shaping our own world. We're just not quite sure how to go about it. We can start with standing firmly in the truth. The truth is, we have to start somewhere.

There is no need to panic! This is not a call for a ban on technology — *you can still have your phone*! This is a plan to have your devices *serve you*, instead of you being a servant to the connection industry. This is a plan intended to empower and appreciate the human part of the emotion-based communication experience. It can even lead to greater self-reliance, self-esteem, peace of mind, self-confidence, personal development, creativity, intuition, increased emotional intelligence, intimacy, professionalism, understanding of others and *being* understood by others, less unnecessary drama, and less embarrassment.

SIANI SYSTEM

The philosophy is to look at the world we're in, to understand that our digital devices are here to stay, and to incorporate technological advances in the connection economy in a way that serves authentic human values. In other words, *people first*. We also need to empower ourselves to reject new technologies that do not serve us well.

You might read this and notice that most of the six principles that follow are just simple common sense. Some of them are hundreds of years old. However, remember that it's very human to know something intellectually and not be able to deal with it emotionally. We also need to be sensitive to the fact that everyone except those who grew up in the past two decades has had the luxury of clear boundaries and protocol.

One — The Human Condition

Embrace authenticity in humanity, collectively and individually. Our needs, desires, and authentic communication process in our relations with one another are critical for our human development. We must be mindful of our purpose. Our interaction habits have a collective effect on us individually and as a society. We must remain mindful of the communication choices we make.

Two — Know That Media Shapes Us

Build a greater awareness of the mediated messages and impact of consumerism on our society. As members of a society, we are members of the "connection industry." The message that we are *mostly* exposed to today is that we "need this thing" to "connect." Become a more discerning media consumer. Identify the "buy this now" message, and be more mindful of being a target for product revenue.

Three — The Effects of Our Digital World

Embrace the truth in light of the research on what our digital devices have been doing to us. 24/7 connecting is not a balanced way to live in our human experience. Adopt the *Embrace* and *Let Go* paradox. We can embrace the positive aspects of technology while still letting go in order to live authentically. If it doesn't feel right, it's not.

Four — Talking and Listening

Establish a commitment to the reeducation of basic communication and social skills. If "having a conversation" is respected as a way to improve our social issues and relations, it's important to model and teach the principles of a productive conversation. Clarify what it means to "connect" in the 21st century. Understand that most of our needs are actually being met when we use our human apps.

Five — The Digital Cleanse

Get to know yourself and the authentic world you live in. Take a personal assessment, and identify and recognize your personal relationship with your digital devices. Do you really know how dependent on technology you are? Incorporate more technology-free interactions into your daily routine in order to build your personal communication skills.

Six — Tools of Transition

Follow an established protocol. Stop and think about the connections you're making, asking yourself "Is this connection personal or impersonal?" We're human, and we can only manage and handle a limited number of relationships. We have to weigh the demands that each of these connections makes on us. Chapter 11 contains a visual tool, the "Siani Steps," that will help you think through all the communication tools and communication options we have, being mindful that the *medium* we choose also sends a message.

LIVE HUMAN

We have banks telling us to "bank human" and Skype telling us to "talk human." How about we actually start to "live human" again? We are walking around wired. The ear bud/head phone culture we have created has cultivated a society where we selectively avoid the people we make physical contact with every day. When we are digitally somewhere else, we are simply not in the real world. This might not seem like a big deal, but making little connections with others throughout the day grounds us in humanity. In contrast, experiencing life through a digital bubble separates us from humanity.

In order to reverse this trajectory, we need to either rediscover or develop our authentic communication skills, which will in turn boost our self-confidence. If for some, communicating with our thumbs has been a primary tool for social interaction, it's going to take time and a little adjusting to build our personal communication skills. One of the reasons some people are reluctant to the idea of even slightly limiting the use of their devices is that they feel threatened by the idea of having to do their personal connections on their own. Two generations have become so used to some sort of filter between themselves and another human being that thinking about face-to-face communication produces anxiety.

When you don't feel that you're good at something, you don't want to do it. That's where practicing comes in. We have to include more Technology-Free Interactions, or TFI's, for a healthier life and better connections.

Just as we know that eating fruits and vegetables is a healthy choice, we need to know that more TFI is healthy for our minds, bodies and souls. The TFI balance starts with your own interactions.

Now is the time to make up for some of the lessons you might have missed as we spent the last two decades distracted by those shiny objects.

> **Try This**
>
> Just for *one day*, try going to work or school free of all technology. Can you make contact with someone with a quick look, a little smile, or by asking, "How's it goin'?" Are you even able to? Or do you feel like you live in Zombieland, where everyone is in their own digital bubble? How does it feel when you get a smile from someone?

CONNECTING

"Connecting" is clearly one of the most overused words in the digital age, right up there with "friend" or "share." When we're talking about human interactions, we cannot use the term "connecting" to mean everything from sexual intimacy or an intimate friendship to hitting the "like" button about your local news team or your favorite cereal. There are different levels of "connecting," and it's vitally important that we distinguish the new connotations of the words that we have adopted into our language. We must educate the younger demographics, whose radar is highly activated to respond to suggestions of social digitally-enhanced connections, that "connecting" on a personal level is not the same as "connecting" in today's digital universe.

Our communication and Internet options are *both* positive and negative. We can find more clarity and also more confusion, more information and more misinformation, more social connections and more feelings of isolation. Social media can bring people together and tear them apart. Our smartphones can educate us and dummy us down. Texting can be a useful tool and a deadly distraction.

What we do know is that our devices are tools, and every tool has a different function. Each tool elicits a different human behavior. If you are on a stage, you communicate differently than if you were on a date. Like a digital stage, Facebook and social media sites are used mostly as an opportunity to make a public impression. Even if you swear that a social connection is just between you and another person, just by the fact that you are capable of reaching hundreds, thousands, millions, you are going to "act" differently. You need your digital stage guidelines, and you need your intimacy building skills, and you need everything in between.

Authentic connections begin and end with personal communication skills. As smart as a smartphone can be, it cannot do the talking for you, or the listening and mental processing. Those are the most important elements in the communication process, and as predicted by a brilliant student six years ago, "When we start communicating with our thumbs, we're in trouble." We now know he was right.

TALKING & LISTENING 101

As I continue to refer to the smartphone as the ultimate enabler when it comes to personal communication skills, it's easy to see why so many people now feel uncomfortable with just initiating small talk. One of the byproducts of our increase in digital connectivity is the heightened difficulty we have with forming and maintaining intimate relationships. As one girl explained, "I have so many friends who think they're *in a relationship* with someone because they have been texting and Facebooking. But then they show up and meet in person, and it's over after the first meeting." Relationships and their development are crucial parts of life for college-age young adults. I've had many students confide, "I don't know where to start [when it comes to talking]" or "What the heck do you even say?"

The enabling aspect of texting means that we never have to evolve from the elementary school "passing the note" phase of communication. I remember writing some silly note as a second-grader — "check Yes or No if you like me" — and physically "sending" it across the room. Then I'd desperately try not to look at the boy reading the note. I waited, and then he would answer and "send" it back. If the answer was No, you can bet he'd be looking straight ahead, too afraid to deal with the emotional accountability of his answer. If it was Yes, I'd be to lucky to catch a glimpse of the corner of a mouth moving into a smile — while he'd still be looking straight ahead. Authentic human-to-human interactions have a way of being indelibly stored in our psyche. Our digitally filtered interactions don't have the same memory building effect.

"I *have* to text all day," said a 20-something student when we started out a class by identifying what kind of communicators the students were. "What do you mean, you *have* to...like you're required to?" I asked. "No, I just mean I have to *talk* to my friends all through the day," she explained. "But, that's not talking, that's exchanging data or information" I said. She corrected me by explaining, "Well, for us, it *is* talking."

Our technology has totally changed the way we communicate with one another and has sent a universal message to an entire generation that there is no need or value in having an authentic conversation with another person. This trend started over six years ago, and our society has simply accepted it.

"How do you measure something that is cultivated?"
— George Gerbner, Media Scholar

It's ironic that the solution to every social problem, political issue, relationship development, or family conflict revolves around the need to "start the conversation." And yet, for almost a decade now, we have been cultivating an entire generation to avoid oral communication. Just as the word "connecting" is now used too broadly, the word "conversation" is also used to include mass communication, meaning that if people are "blogging, posting, and tweeting" they are being "part of the conversation." Personal conversation requires much different skills, and those are the skills that we have forgotten to hone and master and teach the next generation. The nuances we learn to recognize in a personal conversation allow for the development of skills we need for problem solving, professional interactions, personal connections, and intimacy building.

A TYPICAL CONVERSATION

"So, why do you text instead of just talking to your friends at the end of the day and catching up with them?" I asked. "Well, they might need me or I might need them, or I want to tell them something right away," she explained. "So, you don't think you'll remember?" I continued. "Well, sometimes...but, really if I text all day, then I *don't have to talk*, I mean it just takes so much time and sometimes I'm busy, and I just don't have the patience, you know," she said, starting to get a little frustrated with my personal curiosity. "You make talking to a friend sound more like a chore, like something you avoid doing, is that what you're saying?" I asked. "Ah, yeah, it does kinda feel like a chore," she admitted, almost embarrassed with the realization.

"Judging from the silence and the looks on your faces," I continued, addressing a class of about 15 kids, "it seems like this is something you can relate to." Heads nodded sheepishly. "So, what did I miss...when did talking to your friends become more of a chore rather than something you love?" Awkward silence filled the air until one student said, "Whoa, that's heavy."

So we got into an honest conversation about the importance of verbal communication. People connected and felt validated. Others admitted to having the same feelings. I heard the expression, "Oh my God, I thought I was the only one!" repeated a few times. Other remarks included ways to avoid talking to people — claiming that the phone was lost, it got wet, or the batteries died mid-conversation — and confessional chatter along the lines of "Yeah, I know, I do that all the time!" Students were laughing and goofing on each other and bonding in an authentic way, smiling at each other, facing each other, debating and challenging and questioning each other. "So, how did that feel, you guys?" I asked.

They were all much happier now and chuckling with responses like "OK, we get it" or "I see what you did there" or even, "OK I know it's important to talk to people face-to-face, but I'm still not giving up my texting!"

The mere idea that for an entire generation, talking and listening to one another are burdens is not just sad; it's damaging and scary. When I hear parents or teachers saying "How do they not know how to...?" we should be reminded that this is how this group has been socialized. Even if they got these lessons at home, they still missed out. Social interaction may start at home, but it's developed and matured through interactions with their peers and outside the home.

When we start the conversation on the importance of talking and why verbal communication cannot be thought of as an antiquated form of connecting, students respond with, "Yeah, we get it...you need tone and emotion...and with texting you don't get that...you never get the sarcasm...and then you get in trouble...then you have to explain..." They make other comments like "I know that texting can take so much longer then just saying things." However, they are surprised to learn that talking and listening are vital components of human development and mental health.

> "Perhaps one did not want to be loved
> so much as to be understood."
> — George Orwell, *1984*

The words have to come out of your mouth. That's what I mean by talking. We might be posting and blogging and texting and digitally transferring our thoughts with the ability to delete, but this is not the same *process* we go through in face-to-face conversation. In both options, we have to encode our thoughts internally for meaning and scan our mental data for the right words. However, in oral delivery, both conscious and subconscious meanings are shared spontaneously. The nuances of visual and nonverbal cues that we pick up in a face-to-face conversation guide and direct us for the proper responses.

This process is particularly important for young people, whose brains are still developing. The more time we spend using a keyboard to communicate, the less time we have to develop an important skill that will get us what we're really looking for — to be understood, acknowledged, and validated. We need ***constant practice*** in order to accurately articulate our thoughts. Oral communication actually shapes the brain, building a sort of muscle memory in our circuitry, which then allows us to speak spontaneously and more easily. Many young people wonder why they get so nervous and tongue-tied when they have to converse orally. It's because they never properly developed their oral skills, relying instead on their thumbs to do their conversing.

Talking is an important part of self-expression. It's an important part of demonstrating your knowledge, intelligence, sense of humor, wit, personality, and professionalism and of forming and developing your own identity. The way we sound when we "talk" is an enormous part of who we are. Our accents, the quirky way we say certain words, a pause, the rhythm we use, the volume, the clarity, the tone — these all contribute to our uniqueness. These are some of the things that develop our individualism. They also help people to remember you. When my niece was off on her own exploring Europe, she told me "I would start to do something and I could 'hear' Mommy's voice in my head asking 'Do you really think that's a good idea?' and it would make me think twice." A text just does not have the same power.

It can be very scary to "be put on the spot." We've all been there. We go to say something and find ourselves stumbling for the words. Then we cave in to the "Know what I'm saying?" banter until we just give up. Then we feel like idiots; we beat ourselves up and vow never to embarrass ourselves again. The easy solution is to think, "I'll just shut up or text it." Because we can.

When we keep using the devices, which enable us to get out of having to do things for ourselves, we become more and more dependent on our *devices* rather than on our*selves*, which then contributes to our lack of self-esteem. Every time we do something that we thought we couldn't do, we gain confidence. Personal communication is a learned skill and therefore must be used in order to be developed.

Having the words come out orally helps us process our thoughts. It's why "talking through an issue" is a way of resolving problems. Have you ever seen a comedy bit where a patient enters a therapy session and just rambles on for an hour without the therapist saying a word, until the patient resolves all his problems just by hearing his own voice? It is remarkable to observe someone resolve a personal issue or come to a decision just because they verbalized their thoughts in front of another person, or within a group of other people, who did nothing but smile, or nod, or offer some simple look of support.

Use your words.

Words are powerful. How we use those words...even more powerful. We incorporate our words into language to influence, nurture, collaborate, resolve, and be understood. It's like building an inner arsenal of secret weapons. President Lincoln spent days, weeks, and sometimes months agonizing over just the right word to convey a very specific meaning, and look what he was able to accomplish with the "right words."

Try This

Note...many of my students have asked me *not to share* this little trick with you, saying "Well, if everyone knows it, it won't work for me anymore." For one week, when you find yourself asking someone for something, use the phrase "would you mind" in a sincere way. Remember: use the word "would," not "do." Let me know what you experienced.

_____

_____

_____

_____

_____

_____

When people say, "I'm not good at small talk," their problem is not knowing some of the tricks. Before you even attempt to talk, you need to have it in your mind that you are interested in the other person. If your attitude is that everyone you talk to has to entertain you in the first few seconds or you'll be bored, it won't work. Talking is more about thinking. If you want to be interesting, you have to be interested in others.

"If you allow negativity to pervade in your mind, you will produce that negativity with your mouth. Your mouth is the mechanism that reveals how you care for your mind."
— Iyanla Vanzant

People are fascinating. I recently had a conversation with a man who came to my house to repair my clothes dryer. We discussed everything from marital affairs (he has had to fish out a few wedding rings that ended up in pants pockets) to his unconventional upbringing and his work in the music industry. His story would make an incredible movie. The point is, everyone has a story. We make judgments about people. But when we start asking them questions about themselves and hear their stories, we often find that people are quite remarkable.

In some classes we do a version of "Facebook-Live" as a way of introducing ourselves. When people say, "I wouldn't know what to say," I remind them to think about what's on their "profile." "If that's what you're telling the world about yourself, how about feeling comfortable enough to tell the person sitting a foot away from you?" Inevitably, we all end up laughing because everyone's first impressions are so far from reality. Classmates find out interesting things about each other that they wouldn't have learned on a social media site. It's an eye-opening, bonding experience for them.

It's human nature to "like it" when people are interested in you. So, logically, people will like you when you show an interest in them. The basics of small talk are obvious: where are you from...how'd you get here...what are you working on...can I buy you a coffee. And then try some commonalities, such as "name the top five romantic comedies of all time"..."most powerful superhero"..."top five lead singers in bands..."

What's interesting is that as often as I hear people say that they find it hard to just start a conversation with someone, I also hear them say it feels weird if someone approaches them and attempts to start a conversation with them. They feel "It's weird" because they wouldn't know what to say. The "art" of a good conversation is unfortunately becoming lost in the new world of digital communications. We need to bring it back, value it, and cultivate it in our children and young adults.

Try This

Next time everyone is hanging out, turn off all phones and put them away for one hour. See who has the best "conversation starters" of all your friends. You can vote and give the winner a prize. If you find you're getting stuck, there are these great books called *If, Questions For The Game of Life*. There are two volumes filled with all sorts of "if you could, if you had..." You can use some of these conversation starters in your bag of tricks the next time you find yourself in an awkward situation. Then, reflect. How did it feel? What did you learn?

_____

_____

_____

_____

_____

_____

If people find talking difficult, listening is even more of a challenge.

LISTENING

Listening is one of the most powerful communication tools you can develop. In all the relationships you encounter in your life — romantic, friendship, family, business — the most productive communication skill you can use to enhance and enrich these relationships is the ability to listen and validate another human. When someone feels like they are authentically being heard and understood, whether it's personal or professional, that relationship will deepen.

When you ask people to "listen to me," you're really saying, "I need you to understand me." Acknowledgment from others is really the objective. Listening skills should be taught as part of our standard education curriculum. Understanding the importance of active and empathetic listening is one way to create positive results to many of today's social issues.

> "We live in a society where we are more preoccupied with our phones than with each other."
> — Brady Quinn, statement about the suicide of Kansas City Chief Jovan Belcher

Listening is healing.

Cases of depression in our society continue to increase year after year. According to the CDC, "Depression is the leading cause of disability in the United States for individuals ages 15–44." Meanwhile, we know that pharmaceutical medications are big business, and since we're only one of two countries (New Zealand is the other) that allow prescription medication to be advertised, we will continue to receive the message that medication is the answer for depression. However, study after study confirms that the best solution for clinical depression is the combination of *both* talk therapy and medication. When we don't feel like someone "gets us" or understands how we're feeling, we feel lonely. But whether the problem is full-blown depression or just feeling sad and misunderstood, the process of talking to another person has been found to be both healing and beneficial to our mental well-being. There are enormous benefits to our psyche when we have someone who will just listen to us.

The flipside — being a sounding board for friends, family and colleagues — is also beneficial. I talked about this earlier in the book, and because it is so important and is a big part of the solution to our miscommunications, it is important to repeat. Listening is love. When you listen to someone, you tell them that they matter enough for you to give them a little of your time and energy. In our careers as well, actively listening to the people you work with improves your professional image. Take the time to paraphrase what they're saying, clarifying with "So let me make sure I understand you."

In your relationships, instead of trying to "fix" your friend's issues and problems, practice listening in an empathetic way. Use phrases that mirror their emotion. For example, say, "Oh my God, that absolutely sucks. Being stood up is such a horrible experience. I'm so sorry." You don't have to even say anything about yourself or feel like you need to top someone's bad situation; just "feel" for them.

This is a little tougher for men, since the male is wired for "fixing." You may find your male friends anxious to offer the "You know what I would do…" solution. Just listen.

So many of our issues could be resolved if we only stopped to listen to one another. On TV news programs, groups with opposing viewpoints argue as a moderator attempts to host an honest debate of the issues. But each side is committed to pushing its own agenda, spreading its talking points, and, as they say in politics, staying "on message." It is not a conversation if listening is not part of the equation.

There are some good examples of modeling how to have a conversation, but very few examples for the target demographic that needs to learn this skill the most. Reality TV shows receive the highest viewership from the coveted 18- to 24-year-olds. A good conversation, with people clarifying and listening to one another, cannot come close to getting the ratings that knock-out, screaming, table-flipping behavior receives.

Oprah Winfrey is an example of a person with excellent listening skills. If you watch her interviews, you'll see that she listens to every word. She often follows up with "I hear what you're saying" and then paraphrases. Or, she challenges a comment with "So when you say... do you mean?" That's an example of authentic conversation. Oprah's entire empire is built on the foundation of good personal communication and being interested in people.

When it comes to our personal relationships and conflict resolution skills, most of us get caught up in the "shotgun" method of listening. Since we now know the mantra, *emotions outweigh logic every time,* listening in an emotional context is the hardest way to resolve issues.

"OK, so my boyfriend never listens to me" one girl started to explain. "I'm trying to tell him how I feel and he's just not listening." I asked the 20-something student, "So, when *he's* talking, how are *you* listening to him?" She stopped a minute and thought, "Well, I'm trying to think about what I want to say next." "Exactly," I said. "And, that's what he's doing when you're talking. Instead of listening to each other, you're both just 'reloading,' waiting to take your shot, and that's why the issue keeps going around and around and never gets resolved."

Most of the men say something like, "I know if I let her start talking, she will never shut up, so I just don't say anything." I point out, "What she really needs is for you to understand her feelings. As soon as you actually do that, she can stop trying to get you to understand her and she'll stop talking." One guy responded, "You don't know my girlfriend!" The comment resonated with the rest of the male population of the class.

LOVE, INTIMACY, SEX: PART II

One of the unintended consequences of our digital world revolves around our intimate relationships. Perhaps we're on the verge of defining a new idea of human intimacy. However, as of right now, there are plenty of signs and examples that we're developing a distorted vision of intimate relationships. The bottom line: intimate relationships void of authentic human interaction are called fantasies.

The documentary *Catfish* was an eye opener. It showed the shocking online deception of a woman who invented an alternate "self" in order to be a part of a romantic relationship with a young man. The movie was an enormous success. For one thing, we thought that this was a unique and freaky incident. What the documentary more shockingly revealed, however, was just how prevalent and common this behavior had become. The phenomenon is an emerging area of research for those in the mental health profession.

In 2012, Notre Dame football player Manti Te'o referred to "my girlfriend" and "the love of my life" when he publicly announced that he was traumatized by her death. What was shocking and disturbing about this announcement was that Mr. Te'o was referring to someone whom he had never met in person, and that he had been the victim of a *Catfish* scandal. Most people would consider it bizarre that Mr. Te'o referred to someone he had never "met" as his girlfriend, but in the 21st century, digital relationships are quite common. Although being "official" on Facebook is simply not the same as being in a traditionally intimate relationship, matters of the heart will always be profoundly mysterious.

Intimacy can be scary. The level of personal exposure can produce feelings of panic and anxiety, especially for those who don't feel confident in this area. Communicating in the digital world alleviates the social awkwardness many people fear. However, it cannot replace the real-world experiences that are critical for cognitive and emotional development and important for social skills. Building intimate relationships in the real world comes down to courage and practice. The good news is that our brains are malleable. When we start to practice new methods of authentic communication, we can actually rewire the circuitry. The more time teens and young adults spend on practicing good communication skills, the more successful their adult relationships can be.

In the past few years I have started each of my classes with a major disclaimer. I tell my students that we are learning theories and principles of personal communication strategies, so I cannot be held responsible for breakups or hookups. I usually ask my students why they would want to take an interpersonal communication class. A typical response is that they're interested in improving their personal relationships and reaching a deeper level of intimacy.

"I need to get back with my girl," said one student on the first day of class. On the last day of class, he came in, pointed his finger at me and said, "You...I blame you!" He started to smile as I was asking "What?" He continued, "Yup...my new communication skills worked so well, I'm going to be a father!" Other students who practiced some of these basic communication skills with girlfriends and boyfriends told me of marriage proposals and improved family dynamics.

When *I* understand, and *you* understand and *we* understand something *together*, we come to an understanding between *us.* That deepens intimacy. In order to understand each other, we need to communicate in a way that allows for this understanding, and it's not always easy. It takes a lot of practice.

In 21st-century communications, hurtful, cruel, and unnecessary texting, tweeting, blogging, and posting are happening more and more frequently. Miscommunications and disagreements are taking longer to resolve because we are not catching them swiftly enough. Once we hit the "send' button, we lose the ability to control, manage, or take them back.

Fallout is not contained to a small group of friends, because during a Facebook, Tumbl'r, Twitter, or other social media open chat, you're talking to hundreds of people, not just a few. Facebook and social media are being sold as tools of personal communication, when they are, in a very literal sense of the word, broadcasting tools, with an open microphone for everyone.

We were beginning class when I looked at a young man who was clearly stressed out. His face was in his hands. I asked him, "What's wrong?" "You're gonna be mad at me," he said. "I totally went against everything we've been learning in this class." "I am not going to be mad, this is a social science class so we're just here to learn...I won't be mad." He began to explain, "OK, so I got into a fight with my girlfriend on Facebook." As I expected, there were major groans from the class. "Yeah, I know — emotion outweighs logic — I know, I know...but I did it anyway. I was so pissed. But, then, everyone started to get involved and now everyone was taking sides, and then, her mother chimed in..." "Her mother?" I questioned. "Well, yeah, because I'm 'friends' with her mother on Facebook, so now she's going to pull charges for harassment on me..."

We used this as a teachable moment, with students making suggestions on how to handle the situation. We constructed the proper apologies for both the girlfriend and the mother, which had to be made in person, and by the following week things were resolved.

Scenarios like this one are repeated over and over again in social media chat rooms, even to the point where participants are asked to vote on which party is "right." However, in developing intimate relationships or working toward intimacy, being right is not the objective. The objective is to achieve a level of communication in which a greater sense of understanding one another and of meeting each other's needs is met. If one person is the winner, then the other person is the loser — and making someone you care about the loser is not at all loving.

Our smartphones, which have allowed us to be digitally connected to everyone we know, 24 hours a day, seven days a week, 365 days a year, without any universal protocol or boundaries, have been particularly challenging to our intimate relationships. Romantic relationships that once thrived with a call after work, or a buzz before bedtime, now seem to require nonstop texts and constant updates throughout the day. That behavior affects our autonomy, which is a vital part of all intimate relationships.

Try This

For just one week, limit the daily information exchange between you and your intimate partner. For example, no texting what you had for lunch or how boring a teacher is...just save up all that stuff for when you see the person at the end of the day. (Or, save it for a devoted phone conversation.) Remember, conversations are for bonding. The information exchanged is just the material you use to bond. You are sitting and talking with your boyfriend/girlfriend, best friend, in order to share emotions.

REVERSE THE MINDSET

Throughout human history, we've been trying to figure out this phenomenon known as romantic love. The most brilliant minds from the world of philosophy, psychology, technology, spirituality...you name it...will never, *ever,* really be able to thoroughly understand the power of romantic love.

"They are a complete mystery."
— Steven Hawking, theoretical physicist, on women

Over the centuries, we've been able to come up with a list of common denominators to identify feelings of "being in love" and to conceptualize why some types of people fall in love with other types. We try to offer explanations, like "opposites attract." Or we attempt to obtain a better understanding of an individual's psychological pathology in order to explain his or her tendency to end up in a relationship with difficult people. However, we must accept that there is no formula when it comes to emotional love. It cannot be manufactured or bought. Sex, yes...but that feeling of being in love is so enormously powerful, so desirable, and so valuable that it continues to be the driving force in the human experience. People do a lot of crazy things to get "that feeling" and a lot of crazy things to avoid the pain that comes with the loss of that feeling.

The digital world lures us into all sorts of opportunities attempting to fulfill "that feeling." In our instant-gratification culture, we want desperately to believe that along with everything else that is just one click away, being able to fall in love when we want to should be another "instant" benefit of our modern world. But being "in love" is a human emotion. There will never be an app for that.

INTIMACY

The feeling that we long for is more than romance; it's intimacy — true intimacy, between two people. Intimacy can involve anything that we share just between *you* and *me*, something we know about each other, a shared personal memory, something only *you* and *I* do, just between us. Intimacy is a bonding between two souls that can be parent-child, sister-to-sister, brother-to-brother, or friend-to-friend. The level of intimacy depends on the *level of trust* between two people. The deeper the trust, the deeper the intimacy. The capabilities of our digital socialization have dictated and changed our definitions of what it means to be in an intimate relationship.

Be careful. Intimacy and romance have a way of removing all logic. It's just the nature of that part of our human experience. When it comes to romantic love, our hearts and souls are extraordinarily vulnerable. They always have been and they always will be. That's the hard part of being authentically human and is why it's so important to reevaluate our definition of "connections" and to thoroughly understand the impact of our technology when it comes to love.

For an entire generation of people who have been socialized in the 21st century, having access to another person 24/7 through technology has totally redefined what it actually means to be in a relationship. Many social media and smartphone users feel that they're expected to post their relationship activities like a play-by-play announcer at a sporting event. It might be time to embrace the traditional value of privacy when it comes to romantic relationships.

OLD ADVICE FOR THE NEW WORLD

When I was first married, I would call my mother to bitch and complain whenever I had a fight with my husband. She would listen empathetically, feeling sad that I was upset but never acknowledging my comments that he was being "such an asshole." I wanted her on my side, so I'd ask, "Mom, why aren't you agreeing with me?" And she would reply, "Because in two hours you'll be kissing and hugging each other and all you'll remember is that I called your husband a jerk, and you'll be mad at *me*." She was right.

Living out your romantic life out in public leads to more drama than any one person should be expected to handle.

Jeff, Media Lit student, 2013

"I just asked my girlfriend out. And, I guess she posted it on her Facebook status right away. So, then I get a text from my friend asking me why I didn't change my status, because his girlfriend is friends with my new girlfriend. I was like, 'Dude, I just asked her out.' It was like an insult to everyone if I didn't have my status updated like that instant!"

I was having an after-class conversation with three students on love and relationships in the digital age. Jeff was telling more of his story when I noticed one of my students, Brendon, taking out his phone. I asked Brendon, "Are you texting someone a message while we're all here having this conversation?" He replied, "No, I just deleted my Facebook." "Oh, the app on your phone?" I asked. "No, the whole thing. I've been thinking about doing it for a long time, and now I'm convinced. This is ridiculous."

And what about the breakup? We do some pretty stupid things when it comes to losing love. Saying something to someone in the heat of the moment is one thing; however, technology and raw emotions can be a horrible combination. The capability that our technology has for personal attacks and public humiliation can be excruciating.

> "You called me a bitch on the Internet Mark...as if every thought that tumbles through your head was so clever it would be a crime not to share...the Internet is not written in pencil you know..."
> — Aaron Sorkin, writer, *The Social Network*, 2010

It's one thing to have to process a hurtful breakup in private, but a whole new concept when the details are public. Breakups take time to heal, and if we continue to pick at a wound, we constantly delay the healing process. Many people become obsessed with tracking the activities of their exes. I've talked to people who decided to take a quick look at their ex's Facebook status only to learn that the ex is now in a new relationship. The result is painful heartbreak all over again. Are our convenient devices worth the heartache they also create?

We've now had two generations of young people who have gone through adolescence and who have developed in a totally different way than previous generations. We often forget that these young people actually don't have a frame of reference for experiencing their interrelationships any way other than the digital version of life. What they do know is that something just doesn't feel *right*.

THE DIGITAL CLEANSE

In 2010, singer-songwriter John Mayer found himself in a public relations nightmare. After a series of disparaging comments from various interviews in *Rolling Stone* and *Playboy*, along with a few mindless tweets that spiraled out of control, Mayer was dealing with a pretty damaged image. Mayer decided to unplug for a while to, as he explained to Blink 182's Mark Hoppus, "get my head together."

Mayer said, "Stage one of getting my life back together is getting rid of Twitter; stage two is getting a Verizon flip phone, and eventually, doing away with text. Because, I feel like, if you make someone have to call you, most people will never call you." We often forget that celebrities are human. They say stupid things that are documented and then not forgiven. But now these issues aren't restricted to celebrities, since we are all capable of publicly broadcasting our every thought. The comments we express in the spirit of "sharing" can become indelible, nonretractable, subject to personal judgments and misinterpretation on a grand scale. Not unlike the rest of us, Mayer needed a little down time. However, trying to defend his plan against misinterpretation, he went on to explain, "I didn't want to make any broad statements about society, I just didn't want to do it anymore." Should we really "share everything," as the Verizon slogan states?

Mayer's "need to get my head together" got me thinking about how my students would deal with the same type of digital cleanse. Because I was teaching a social science class, one in which students learn about human behavior in the society we live in, how would they feel about living without their digital devices? The initial reaction was not positive.

In 2009–2010, we were not using the word "addiction" in discussing digital devices — at least not in any serious tone. But when students reacted to the thought of being without a phone, their lack of self-reliance and the shift of tone and expression into anxious behavior were revealing.

Ben's story:

"When I first signed up for the class, it was basically because I saw who was teaching it. When I first sat down in the class and Joni mentioned this so call 'digital cleanse' business, I turned to [my friend] Jackie sitting next to me and said 'That sounds like bullshit.'"

As I explained the digital cleanse I was watching for reactions. There were many stunned faces and quite a few students turning to each other and mumbling comments, so I asked for feedback. "What do you think? Is this something you could do, or want to try? What exactly is your biggest concern?"

Some students got visibly nervous, asking, "So, seriously, what do you mean? Like, we can't talk to anyone for a week?" Or, "What about work and what about if we got into a car accident and didn't have our phones on us?" And then there were the "no way" people, with comments like "There is no way I could do that, I mean, I'm a mother, I have to be able to stay in touch with my kids." Or, "There's no way I could do that because that's the only way my boss gets in touch with me." (I came to find out later that the comments that students made after they walked out of the classroom and out of my hearing range were more along the lines of "She's totally fucked…she has no idea what it's like to communicate today…she has no idea about how we need to use Facebook to connect…she's totally out of touch with how to communicate today…")

Despite the incredulous looks, fear, and verbal pushback, I could also see the wheels of curiosity spinning in the minds of these future social scientists. "Look," I said, "you're in a social science class and the subject is interpersonal communication. That means that you're supposed to be able to study human behavior in the way that we communicate on a one-to-one basis. This is not mass communication, where we study how mediated messages reach the general public, this is about how *you* are communicating with those close to you. And, at a time when we have totally changed the models for that form of communication!" I went on to explain that the two previous semesters had turned into hours of Facebook and Tumbl'r therapy, so it seemed pretty evident to me that this generation was not getting their personal communication needs met.

"So, let's just experiment." I explained, "This is about collecting information and not about whether or not you have the will power to remove yourselves from the digital world." (Of course, finding out that they might **not** be able to is as revealing and informative as if they could do it.)

Some students were anxious to jump at the chance and very excited, saying right away "Oh, I'm totally going to do this," while others took weeks to warm up to the idea. The common denominator was curiosity, with many students saying some form of "I think I'd like to know if I could?"

Ben continues:

"Slowly but surely, as every class progressed with assignments, the 'social scientist' in us complained and criticized on how communication with technology was negatively affecting our personal lives. Though I understood the idea why texting and tweeting made me personally distant from my close friends and family, I had to experience communicating without this technology to mentally grasp what it was actually doing to me."

Together, we came up with a social science experiment to expose how the communication tools of the 21st century are affecting our interpersonal relationships and our own relationships with our digital devices.

Objectives

* To see how it ***feels*** to connect with people without the tools of our 21st-century communication devices

* To personally discover whether these devices are improving our personal relations or compromising them

* To find out whether students *feel* more understood or less understood

* To find out what students are afraid of

* To find out whether students will *feel* more anxious or less anxious

* To find out whether students are addicted — in other words, do they actually *feel* like they can live without it?

* To find out how students feel about our world of 24/7 connections

Together we came up with the guidelines, which we basically turned into what could be considered a week of living in the 1960s "Mad Men" era.

The Rules

For one week, students had to eliminate their digital technology. That means no Internet, no Facebook, no social media, no tweets, no Google, no cell phone with them all day or in the car. Many students said that they no longer had a landline, so "does that mean we can't talk to anyone for a week?" We decided to treat the cell phone as if it was a landline — only for talking, no texts. It had to be plugged into a wall so it was "wired" and students had to stay in the room to talk to someone.

This also meant no email and — the biggie — no iPod! "No iPod...oh my God!" one student screamed. "I'm gonna have to listen to my own thoughts...I swear, I will not be able to do that!!" "Well," I responded, "won't that be revealing! You might have some really interesting thoughts...you might get really creative!" "No," he said, "I will probably go insane!" "Oh my God...what about games? Some of us are 'gamers.'" Another student jumped in with "No, no games. They didn't have video games in 1965!"

So, we determined that students could go to a movie, watch broadcast television, write a letter, leave notes, and visit in person. As we discussed the logistics of this assignment, quite a few students were concerned about the idea of face-to-face meetings: "Oh my God, are we really supposed to just walk up and knock on somebody's door...that is going to be totally weird...that is going to creep my friends out."

The Journal

The next part of the assignment was for students to keep a daily record of how they were *feeling* and how their lives were being affected without 24/7 digital connectivity. We wanted to get the answer to some of the fears of "being left out" or "missing out." The anagram FOMO was not even referred to when we started the cleanse, but the condition and behavioral signs were revealed as students anticipated their participation. The room echoed with panicky cries of "What if someone is trying to get in touch with me?" I found it fascinating that they didn't believe there was any alternative.

Because we had quite a number of film students, students suggested that it would be cool if we could use a camera to document this exercise. "Well, they did have cameras in 1965," one student pointed out. Considering that many of our real feelings are expressed nonverbally, and that our nonverbal communication is spontaneous and revealing, we decided that filming the daily journal would be an option. That way we could see and analyze the effects.

The Results

"I haven't been on Facebook for a whole week now. I feel so much better!"
— Student who took part in our "digital cleanse," 2011

I have heard many versions of that during my discussions with those who have tried to "back off for a while." They also admit that they "feel better" when having to go a day without a phone. The language that students use reminds me of people who have stopped drinking or gone through a period without caffeine. The question is, if you're feeling better because of self-imposed digital restrictions, how do you feel when you're immersed in the constant connectivity?

"The Digital Cleanse was not what I expected. I can honestly say that I have not had a single issue with no texting and no social networking. I realize the lack of communication (between people)…you really get a perspective of how rude it (texting) is when you see others doing it."
— Jackie, day three of Digital Cleanse

In the course of three semesters between 2010 and 2011, roughly 75 students participated in this informal social science experiment. The consensus was that doing a digital cleanse for one week was informative and highly revealing on many levels. For students, the most important part was learning about their relationship with technology. The most repeated sentiment was "It was eye-opening."

> "By completing the digital cleanse project, I found that I was a technical zombie within a sea of others. Just absorbing what my phone tells me and where to go. Now I find myself leaving my phone at home because the people I go out with are more important then checking Twitter, Tumbl'r and Facebook."
> — Billi, Fashion Retail Management Student, 2012

For those who said, "I already know I'm addicted, I know I can't do it," even making an attempt revealed their compulsive relationships with their devices. Their reflection papers and video journals were a collection of "Well, I tried again today, and it was really, really hard." One student explained, "I tried to walk out the door without it and had to turn the car around and go back in and get it. I was really panicking."

Even for students who were confident that they *could* succeed at the digital cleanse, actually testing that assumption was revealing. Many students reported that they just hadn't realized how many times they reached for their phone throughout the day until they didn't have it with them.

Back to Ben:

"I'm going to be honest. I thought the whole time I could do this 'cleanse' with such ease and that I didn't need a phone or Internet to stay connected with the world. I'm admitting my first three days I felt that this was wrong. The first three days were the hardest, not even the fact that I wasn't using my phone to text but that I didn't have it on me at all times. I felt like an addict going through withdrawal. I know that sounds crazy, but having a phone, not in my pocket, I felt like a piece of me was absent, almost like a security feature to tell me, ok, keep walking. I found myself a lot of the times, walking to the bus stop and abruptly halting in the middle of the sidewalk feeling anxious about having empty pockets. Day four I reconnected with my close friends through phone calls, and checking in with them throughout the week and even making plans to hang out [with them] without texting or Facebook! [Before this experiment] I truly didn't think it was possible to get in touch with some people without texting because of the awkwardness that may occur since we only text on a day to day basis."

Many of the students who went through this "eye-opening" experience learned so much about themselves and the world around them that they were anxious to share their experiences with their family and friends. They became "communication converts," understanding that "connecting" in order to feel more fulfilled has to be done on a human level.

"Since my digital cleanse, I have been able to pick up my phone and just call my Dad. We have always had a bit of a distant relationship...now we have had many short conversations on the phone instead of texting one or two things back and forth...[people] don't think they need real life contact."
— Student, 2012

During our conversations and reflections on what they learned about the nuances of personal communication, many have said they actually feel "deceived" and "used." "It's really like they're lying to us...I mean, it's [technology] just not going to give you what we really need, ya know" said one student during a casual chat after a class.

Many schools have been trying to initiate gadget-free days or digital downtime experiments without much success.

If digital connectivity has an addictive component for some people, then you can't expect a person who is physically and emotionally reliant on something to just stop using it. A level of compassion and understanding needs to accompany a cleanse. It's important to try to understand what they're going through and how they're feeling, and to know what we can do to help if they are feeling scared.

It's also important to give students alternative tools before initiating the digital cleanse experiment. We spent weeks building the skills beforehand, reeducating students with the foundational communication skills of talking and listening, and *experiencing* the benefits of authentic human connections. Everyone can benefit from learning the best ways to articulate thoughts, speak with confidence, listen with interest, and practice active and empathetic listening. As each new group had the time to build and practice their skills before the week-long digital cleanse, they were actually "pumped" to try it.

Most students found the digital cleanse "empowering." A common thread was that they had a great deal of new confidence, their relationships improved, and they honestly "got" that personal communication is much more than they had thought. They seemed to value other people more and found out how much they really "hate" their digital world. Many students have deleted their Facebook accounts, saying, "I can't believe how stupid it really is" and "People just don't get it."

Attempting to close a Facebook account can be difficult, as Facebook's emotional taunting can be too hard to resist. "Are you sure you want to leave? Your 'friend' Diane is going to miss you." This is blatant emotional manipulation, motivated by the fact that each person's page is a valuable asset for stockholders.

Some close their Facebook accounts and then feel "forced" to reopen them, because they feel left out. Many companies entice users with prizes and deals. Schools set up pages for clubs and activities as a convenient way to post information. The left-out feeling is legitimate. People are listening to friends talking about things they missed by not participating. The fact is, we cannot be expected to know everything, and it's important to feel OK about *not* knowing everything.

The digital cleanse gives people who have been using social media as a personal communication tool a frame of reference as to what life feels like without the pressure of nonstop connectivity. Jackie, a student who did the digital cleanse in 2012, has admitted that she struggles with FOMO going back and forth with her technology use. When I ran into Jackie one day, she said to me, "Oh my God, I was just thinking of you, and saying to myself, Oh my God, I really need another cleanse!"

The Collective Results

Students submit a written reflection of their experience. One thing they all agree on is that there is a reduction in their stress, and they all realize how much time they "waste." Some admit that they "have all my homework done" and that having "no time" is no longer a viable excuse. Rooms get cleaned and laundry is done.

Many say things along the lines of "I need to live my own life and not get caught up in other people's lives." Many students who have been in the habit of putting ear buds in before walking out the door found it "weird" to experience the world around them authentically. They enjoyed listening to the sounds around them, listening to people's conversations, and being aware of how everyone else is "going through life in their own little bubble world," as one girl said.

Many felt better physically when they didn't have their phones with them or their laptops turned on overnight. One student who thought he had insomnia discovered that as soon as his phone wasn't at arm's length, he actually slept through the night. While watching this student's video diary, the class commented on the change in his physical appearance from the first day to his final day, when he looked happier and had more energy. Many students said they were relieved and happier just focusing on their close friends and family instead of "everyone on the planet." In general, they said that talking just felt better, "more fulfilling," than texting all day. One of the most surprising comments was that many students reported "more confidence" or "better self-esteem." When I asked why, they explained that they felt more capable about their communication abilities and that made them happier.

The change in perspective that the digital cleanse provides is important. However, we know that any successful diet needs to involve a lifestyle change. We're part of a digital world and we have a need to be connected. What we need now is a universal understanding and an established protocol for the tools of our 21st-century communication.

Chapter 11

The Tools of Transition

Living the Don Draper life in the 21st century might be tough. Since the *Mad Men* days of the 1960s, our technology has totally changed our daily expectations of one another. However, we can improve those interactions and create a more sustainable way of interacting if we establish a universally accepted understanding of our human needs, combined with an honest evaluation of how our tools of the 21st century can best be used to meet those needs. When shaping social norms, the best thing to do is start with a general consensus. Since the solution to social issues usually begins with "have a conversation," that's what I did.

THE PHILOSOPHY

The idea behind the Siani System of digital communication is simple. In fact, many positive solutions to our biggest social problems are grounded in simplicity. Researcher Michael Pollan addresses the American obesity issue in his best-selling book *In Defense of Food: An Eater's Manifesto* with the mantra, "Eat food. Not too much. Mostly plants." Can you imagine the problems we could resolve as a society if we all did that? The Siani System is similar to Pollan's philosophy. "Connect with people. Connect with yourself. Mostly authentically." Once we embrace the philosophy, the next issue to address is *how* do we do that in this digitally saturated world with a buffet table full of tempting options?

The Siani System includes helpful tools of transition for a well-balanced, sustainable communication lifestyle. The *Siani Scale* and the *Siani Steps* Model of Communication for the 21st century are based on fundamental principles of interpersonal communication. This system is the result of a consensus reached through individual and group conversations, class work, and personal interviews with teenagers and young adults who, despite regularly using these tools in their own trial-and-error methods, still admitted to feeling unsatisfied and unfulfilled in their personal communication behavior.

The Siani System also serves the business world. When the communication expectations for a professional environment in the 21st century are clearly stated, everyone is put on the same page. Because our communication behavior has rapidly changed in such a short period, businesses and corporations must create very clear guidelines for communication in the digital age. When two generations have been socialized differently than previous generations and there are different definitions of "appropriate," the rules must be clearly stated.

TOOLS OF TRANSITION

"We have to love our technology enough to describe it accurately and we have to love ourselves enough to confront technology's true effect on us."
— Sherry Turkle, *Alone Together*

We need to create a national protocol to readjust our social norms for a healthier society. We've done it before and we can do it now, if we work together. We need to define some boundaries. The word "boundary" is often thought of as negative or as an infringement on our freedom. However, we have to remember that we embrace healthy boundaries and that they are critical in our everyday lives. Remember playing hide-and-seek? Before starting the game, you would establish the boundaries — you couldn't go beyond a certain house, or you had to stay within certain limits. And if you didn't, you were "out of bounds" and not in the game.

Our digital world is an endless universe. Texting, tweeting, hours and hours on social media sites...it's like a party that's never over and that you feel like you can't leave, because you might miss something or someone cool might show up the minute you leave. The reality is that you're totally exhausted and just want to go home and go to sleep. One girl told me that the only way she *can* fall asleep is if she and her friend go back and forth all night texting until "I just pass out."

What is not sustainable is living life on high alert, 24 hours a day, seven days a week. *That* is killing you.

Establish your own personal boundaries of availability. In other words, tell people your schedule. Then nobody has to wonder why you're not getting back in touch with them. "I'll be in classes Monday through Wednesday until 7 P.M., so I'll look forward to catching up on Thursday," or "I'll be doing brain surgery all morning and will return messages after my reality TV show taping." Communicate. Try it with your closest relationships, maybe just your core 10.

Pick a time to shut down for the day and stick with it. Close down your laptop for business interactions at a reasonable workday time, and resume the next morning. Impose limits on your media consumption. Remember, we *know* too much media consumption can make you sick, just as we know that drinking too much alcohol might make you throw up or end up with a hangover. When we consume too much material for our minds to process, we get stressed out or have a mental breakdown.

We have to impose some structure within our nonstop digital world. Boundaries and structure have to be a part of the digital world moving forward.

Actress and new mom Drew Barrymore was on *The View* talking about her life growing up with her "hippie parents," who didn't believe in raising her in a structured environment. And perhaps because of her teenage alcoholism, she said, "I'm not doing that with my child...kids need structure." We all need a sense of structure. Every established society has had the time to develop the rules for existing in a harmonious way where people just know how to "be."

How do we know when we've stepped *over* the lines between private or public, personal or impersonal, professional or casual, friend or acquaintance, business or pleasure? It's time to give some structure to our digital world so we can coexist with a better understanding of our human expectations.

MIND*FUL* NOT MIND*LESS*

One thing we also learned from the Digital Cleanse experiment was how many students were behaving mindlessly. As they explained, "I would open up my laptop to type a paper for homework and realize I was on Facebook. I don't even remember how I got there." Another student confirmed her experience by saying, "I would catch myself typing it [Facebook homepage] in and then say, 'What am I doing?'" For many students, clicking their Facebook icon was a habit. One said, "I thought, 'I'll just do a quick check,' and then, an hour later I was like, 'Oh my God, what just happened?'" Great news for Facebook, but not so great for you.

The cell phone industry is telling us to "talk and surf," "text and talk," and that "doing two things at once is better, right?" in the commercial where a man is talking to a group of little kids. No — not for ALL tasks. This is a terrible message to be sending a culture where people are already so distracted, as one doctor told me, that just about "everyone who takes the online ADHD test is basically diagnosed with the condition."

You might be able to do two things at once if one of those things is considered a "mindless" task. For example, you might be able to peel a potato and chat. However, if you have to stop to read a recipe while chatting, you have to pause the conversation so you can process the information you need to take in.

When Al Roker is talking on *The Today Show* and then they put up someone's tweet for us to read, we will miss what he has to say about the weather. I can hear you disagreeing with me, saying "It's not true. I *can* do two things at once." But research shows it's a misconception that we can mentally multitask, and when we do multitask, the results are usually half-assed.

CONNECTING

People are *not* computer chips. It might be easy to make the comparison when discussing how our brains work. However we are human. For those of us who choose to stay human, embracing our limits can be liberating in a world of digital demands. We should not be *expected* to store endless amounts of data and collect endless "connections." The truth is, we can only handle so many connections. For the past two decades we've been gorging on information and relationships; we've become *mental hoarders* of stuff and people. Just because we can be connected to everyone and everything doesn't mean we should.

It's important to *think* about the connections that we're making. Malcom Gladwell's research shows that we can only handle about 150 relationships, total. When you are constantly bombarded with requests to "Like" me, "Follow" me,

"Connect with" me, it's important to stop, think, and weigh the *value* of the connection while mindfully understanding the *objective* of the connection.

Is someone asking you to connect in order to begin an ongoing friendship, or are you being asked to be an "audience" for someone — part of a fan base, a piece of data that will define your demographic and be used to sell you something, or a way to increase profits for a product? *Why* am I supposed to "like" my cereal or "visit" my eyedrops on Facebook?

It's easy to say Yes to everyone who is asking you to "connect." The word itself plays a psychological game with your head, as it has an emotional connotation. Take a minute to think about what you can handle, and understand that *every* connection that you make is going to require you to *manage* that relationship on some level. If you "like" something with one click, you may spend a lot of time deleting all the new emails that pop up in your in-box.

SIANI SCALE

THINK! Think quality over quantity when you're deciding what to take in. If I am limited to 150 connections, how am I going to manage them? Our personal connections are a valuable source of our personal satisfaction. They should be respected and not lumped in with all of the many impersonal and public connections that consume our time and energy. A few precious gems on one side might weigh less than a ton of crap on the other side, but which would you rather have? Think about weighing each connection based on whether you are making a personal or impersonal connection, and how much the connection is costing you in time and energy.

Siani Scale

We have more tools of personal connection than we could ever have imagined. The issue is that we haven't thought through how these tools are going to affect our communication behavior. We have been focused on what "the tools can do *for* us" rather than what "they're doing *to* us," and how they redefine and shape the interactions and the behavior of the communicator.

As we've been focused on the speed and efficiency of the delivery of the message, have we stopped to consider whether the *method* of communication is actually meeting the objective of our desired connection? We hear "connect" and "fast" and seem to feel that our personal connections can be accomplished with the click of a button. Using words that have an emotional connotation, when in fact the objective is to sell something, can cause disappointment if you're in need of an emotional connection.

THE EROSION OF "PERSONAL"

How the heck are we supposed to communicate on a personal level when we can't even identify and agree on the definition of "personal"? With tweeting, instant messaging, Snapchat, Instagram, Facebook, Skype, a phone call, everyone seems to have their own definitions of what it means to communicate on a "personal" level.

We wonder why young adults and teens are getting in trouble for being "inappropriate" on the job or at school, when we have never defined "appropriate" for them. We've approached these new ways of communicating with the insane idea that "everyone should just know." Well, we don't. If a teenager is sitting with a group of people and texting nonstop, and nobody says, "That's inappropriate," then of course this behavior is going to continue. Some bosses text while talking to their employees, and many parents think it's OK for them to text at the table, while at the same time telling their kids that it's rude.

EVALUATING THE TOOLS

Over a two-year period, in classes, group discussions, and interviews with students, teens, and young adults, we discussed how to categorize our 21st-century communication tools so that we can clearly establish a "best practice" model of application. But before we could evaluate the tools, it was important to agree on what we mean by "personal."

The lines between personal and impersonal have become incredibly blurred over the past decade. Defining the idea of a "personal connection" in the 21st century is subjective, perhaps because a feeling is impossible to measure. Is asking someone to "friend" you considered "personal"? Is calling someone on the phone considered personal or intrusive? What might feel "personal" to one person might feel uncomfortable to another. What one person may find totally "appropriate" may be considered totally "inappropriate" to someone else.

During our conversations, we agreed that in determining whether a communication exchange is "personal" or "impersonal," we have to consider elements such as the level of focused attention, the amount of time and energy you give to the other person, the level of thoughtfulness, the level of vulnerability, dedication to the interaction, and physical attention.

The tools of our digital age have broadened the opportunities for each individual, and have given us the *one-to-one*, *one-to-many*, and *one-to-most* models of communication. On one side, it was a no-brainer to establish the fact that even in this day and age, the traditional face-to-face model still serves as the best method of enabling intimacy and bonding, and forms the most personal connection. On the other end of the spectrum, the tools of mass communication, or *one-to-most* model, can be considered the least personal.

We hashed out all the ways we were communicating with each other and tried to understand the reasons why some methods *felt* personal and others didn't. We went round and round debating whether after face-to-face, a phone call should be next on the level of "personal," or should it be Skype/Facetime because, after all, you can "see" the person? "Oh that's right!" I said. "So, what's the difference?" One fashion student answered, "No, I'm sorry, that's just too weird, to be like holding someone's face in your hand, I just hate that."

As we were trying to figure out the best use of technology for creating the closest possible bond between two people, what I found surprising for the kids of the digital generation was that time, energy, and focus were better qualifiers of "personal" than speed. One student said, "I would love to get a letter from someone." "Really?" I wondered. "More than being able to respond right away?"

I asked this same question about letters and cards to several different groups and always received some variation of, "Well you just know that someone is taking the time and really thinking about you." They also mentioned that seeing someone's handwriting "feels more personal" and that they can save and collect letters. As one student said, "I still have every letter my grandmother wrote to me. I mean, you're not going to feel the same about an email."

One student said, "I actually started sending letters to my girlfriend this year. Now she sends letters to me and we collect them." At a birthday celebration, I met a lovely young 25-year-old woman, Megan, who said that she now tries to send out a letter to a friend or family member, sometimes with a little "care" package, on a regular basis. She explained her reason: "First, to keep the post office alive and those jobs maintained, and then, because it really says that those people are important to you."

In our ambitious goal of making sense of our tools of connectivity, we clearly established that *efficiency* and *personal* rarely coexist. As we know, the medium itself is a message. Regardless of advances in our communication technology, people still crave "personal" connections — connections that say, from the tool you use, "You are worth my time and energy. You are so important to me that I will take five minutes out of my day and call you to hear your voice, or surprise you with a card or note in the mail." Sending your wedding invitation or announcement through Facebook might seem like a good use of modern technology. For someone on the receiving end, however, it doesn't *feel* right. "I'm just like one of a million people who got that same message," one girl explained, "so, I mean, it just didn't feel personal."

There is a place for personal and a place for efficiency. If the objective is to send out a message to a large number of people, mass messages can be an effective use of technology. But in this day and age, defining "personal" can be challenging. If you need a determining factor in order to decide between personal and impersonal, think of this: When you can't see or don't know who is actually receiving your message, that communication method falls under the "less personal" category.

SIANI STEPS

The *Siani Steps* offers a protocol for the tools of 21st-century communication. The *Steps* can be a helpful reminder; they work as a mental graphic organizer for you to consider when you are trying to choose among the many communication options. After you've taken a few seconds to *think* about whether the connection you're about to make is considered personal or impersonal on the large spectrum, it's important to think about *how* personal, *what* is the objective, and what communication *tool* is the right tool to meet the objective.

Face to Face
In person, focused attention; facing/speaking one-to-one; in the same environment; sharing sight, sound, smell, touch, air, energy, vibes, attitude, vulnerability, emotions, real-time feedback

Phone Call/Skype
Focused attention; speaking one-to-one; sharing sound, vibes, emotions, energy, attitude, vulnerability, real-time feedback

Card/Letter Mail
Writing one-to-one; giving time and energy; making your thoughts personal and to be received by only one person

Email One-to-One
Writing to one person directly, through the use of technology; the most acceptable form of business communication; in many circles, the only acceptable way businesses and professionals will take in information; a useful tool when materials and data require documented exchanges and for storing data and contact information; shows time, energy and focus

Texting
Mostly one-to-one, but can be one-to-many; originally intended to be used as a "quick note"; a primary form of communication for many, enabling less personal interactions; texting data can feel "cold" as dialogue is exchanged without salutations

Social Media
(1) Restricted Small Group Communication — Email/Social Media
Receivers of messages are part of a large group; depending on the settings and the number of people in the group, receivers can feel like part of a community or part of the world audience

(2) Unrestricted Posts/Blogs/YouTube/Broadcast/Social Media
For messages to a mass audience; a message has the potential to reach millions in an instant

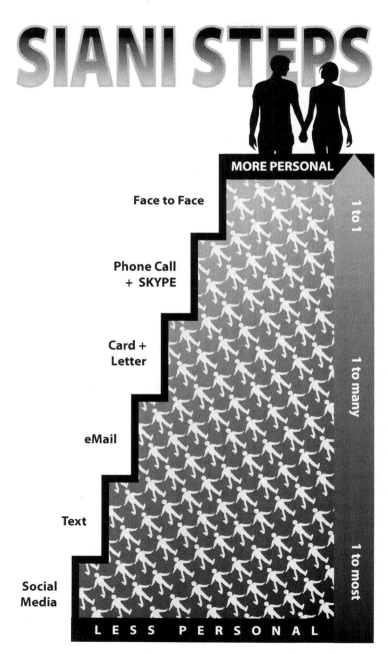

SIANI STEPS

MORE PERSONAL

Face to Face

Phone Call + SKYPE

Card + Letter

eMail

Text

Social Media

1 to 1

1 to many

1 to most

LESS PERSONAL

As we have said, the starting point for any communication connection is knowing the objective. If we can settle on this, for now at least, as a basic protocol of understanding what tools best meet the objective, then we know what we have to do. If the objective is for more personal connections, then we can stop and think and choose to "step up" a little at a time toward making each connection a little more personal. Remember, people's needs haven't changed. Technology did. There are some things in life that technology cannot improve.

The lower steps reflect the *one-to-most* model, and as we go up the steps, to the *one-to-many* and then the *one-to-one*, our levels of intimacy and personal connection increase. Conversely, the *one-to-most* options, when embraced as tools of mass communication, can serve that objective efficiently. When we are honestly describing these tools accurately, understanding their capacities and limitations, and embracing the idea that sometimes the most perfect tool is not a tool at all but a human being, we can start to unravel the love/hate dynamic that we have with our devices.

The digital age has allowed us unlimited opportunities for communication. The top three steps, face-to-face, phone/Skype, and letter/cards, are best when the objective is to build a personal relationship. Whether it's business, family, friendship, or romance, the choice to use any of these one-to-one options sends a *more personal* message. In addition to the time and energy, the top three steps are considered more personal because the sender and receiver clearly understand that the communication exchange is between "us." Knowing that a communication exchange is "just between us" affects the behavior and level of trust and personal disclosure that can enhance the relationship.

Emailing and texting are now considered convenient ways of exchanging information between two people. As smartphones now have Internet capacity, information can be sent and received 24 hours a day, seven days a week, 365 days of the year. These still fall under the one-to-one model, and they can *feel* like they're between two people. But because of the electronic *capabilities,* you can never be absolutely certain that an email or text went *only* to you. Because of that, these mediums affect the communication behavior of both the sender and receiver.

Social media fall under the one-to-most model. Just as your communication behavior is different when you're talking to just one person in front of you as opposed to when you're addressing a group of people, this same shift occurs when you use digital tools. Because communicating through social media involves more people, it is naturally less personal.

Face-to-Face

When we refer to Face-to-Face communication for this model, we are referring to being with another individual or individuals in the same physical space and in a small setting such as a room, office, or restaurant. This is the top tier for personal communication because it offers the greatest opportunity to create the truest personal experience in the communication process. The communication can be positive or it can be negative, but this is the most revealing and most authentic interpersonal communication relationship.

Nothing is more powerful than looking someone in the eyes. That's where true emotions are revealed. In our physical face-to-face space with one another, a host of subconscious messages are being exchanged like rapid fire. They are constant and circular. Scientists, criminal profilers, psychologists, parents, children, doctors, teachers, friends, and lovers can learn more about the person they are with in a fraction of a second with the first glance than through any other communication method.

Meeting the eyes of another person allows us to fall in love, catch a lie, know when someone is in trouble, or understand that someone is confused. I could continue to write pages and pages about the benefits of face-to-face communication, but we already know it's important. We just need to understand and embrace the idea that there is absolutely no form of technology that can substitute for this all-encompassing and important form of communication.

Face-to-face communication must be reinforced as an important value in our human experience. This does not mean just showing up in person; this means showing up prepared to give all your attention to the person in front of you. Face-to-face means that you are giving your time, energy, and full attention to the person you are with, without any other multitasking agenda. Your physical behavior must also say to the other person that you are worth my time, my energy, and my focus and I am going to spend this time just with you.

> *Pew Research Center reports texting as a primary form of communication, with 63 percent of teens texting verses 39 percent calling and talking. However, a study in the* Journal of Evolution and Human Behavior *finds emotion-linked hormones — including cortisol and oxytocin — responsible for regulating stress and enabling bonding, responded positively when girls talked over a stressful event with their mothers compared to when they texted.*

When we consider the increased levels in stress and anxiety among the younger generations, talking is a simple solution. Face-to-face communication involves more than the ability to see facial expressions; it also involves reading and deciphering meaning from the slight nuances of those expressions. It is vitally important for brain development and the development of your emotional intelligence. It is the most bonding of all forms of communication for many reasons.

In physical face-to-face communication, we share sound, tone, energy, smell, touch, vibe, attitude, emotions, and those sexual chemistry signals known as pheromones! All of these personal nuances are *invaluable* to the human experience and need to be recognized as such. If your intention is to build personal relationships, you have to remember that your digital tools were intended to be used *only* when face-to-face communication is *not* an option, and never as an improvement on the real thing. We also have to remember that people tend to get lazy. Sometimes, harder is better. Working hard on our personal communication skills leads to greater fulfillment and a greater sense of accomplishment. When it comes to building intimacy, the easy and efficient route cannot be a viable alternative.

Again, I am not suggesting that we all stay home from work and school and just stare at each other and give each other big hugs all day. We know that we have responsibilities; I'm just saying that if your objective is to be close, feel close, and deepen your relationships, face-to-face communication transcends all inventions and has the time-tested track record to fulfill your personal communication and bonding needs. There is no substitute.

Phone Call / Skype

In the context of interpersonal communications, the next best way to communicate in today's world is a phone call or *possibly* Skype. First, for more than 100 years, the phone call has been the traditional way of communicating interpersonally for those moments when you can't be with someone. It's considered a necessary social skill in the business world and on a personal level. As AT&T's popular "reach out and touch someone" slogan from 30 years ago suggests, it's still an important way to bring people together.

People still need to be heard, and the voice carries subconscious emotions. There is a unique intimacy even in the silence and pauses of a phone conversation. You can pick up on a person's mood and attitude, express aspects of your personality — sarcasm, sense of humor, spontaneity — and for many people a phone call provides just the right amount of privacy to allow a slower yet authentic connection. Instant cues are exchanged within the nuances of a phone call.

Since we don't have any time-tested research with Skype, we cannot conclusively know that it produces any closer communication opportunities than a phone call. Sometimes we're quick to label something new as "better" than what we already have. Video call services, such as Skype or FaceTime, can offer wonderful opportunities for inter-personal communication for certain occasions. However, there are subtle elements and luxuries that you can get in phone conversations that make both communication experiences simply *different.* There are benefits to both and draw-backs to both.

The Skype campaign is interesting, as it promotes the value in "talking like a human." I could have used the entire campaign for promoting this book and replaced "Skype can do that" with "People can do that." If you notice, they don't even showcase anyone using Skype in their advertising campaign; they simply display real people being with real people without any form of technology. That has pretty much been the entire idea of this book.

However, in cases where people cannot be together, Skype has been a remarkable way to connect business associates, families, friends, and lovers across oceans and put them at the kitchen table, and at practically no cost. Long-distance phone calls remain very expensive. However, you can Skype and see people you care about. What we're still cautious about is how we're using Skype.

"Oh my God, I was Skyping with my friend and all he did during the entire conversation was look down at his phone, and he even started texting people!!"
—Student, 2013 Media Literacy

Skype is intended to be used as a tool for the next best thing to face-to-face communication. If that's what we decide it's supposed to be used for, then we have to follow the same level of focus and attention as if we are in the same room with the person. We have to remember that whatever tool we use, the devices themselves have a way of altering our behavior. With Skype, people are still separated by a screen. Also, people are prone to behave differently in front of a camera. If you're trying to give someone your attention and the self-image box on your screen is distracting you, you're naturally going to be self-conscious about the way you look.

The person that you're Skyping with also has a lot to do with your level of comfort while communicating. Some friends have admitted that they wouldn't Skype without makeup on, or that they "perform" a bit in front of the camera. Others have said that it can be really helpful. One international student said that he really likes to use Skype "to talk to my Mom. If I'm on Skype, I feel closer to her because I haven't seen her in a while."

Cards/Letters

The tangibility factor of cards and letters adds a personal touch to the communication process. I was surprised that so many students believed that the traditional written letter would remain a fixture of personal communication. During the interviews and discussions, students' reasoning centered around the *feeling* that "someone cared enough," "took the time," or "thought enough about me." One girl explained, "If someone is writing you a letter and taking the time to get it to the post office, and mail it, you get the feeling that they're thinking about 'me' all during that time. That is definitely different than someone just shootin' off a text." People like personal attention.

There is an emerging trend in marketing today to become more personal. Some agencies are actually hiring teams of people to sit and handwrite envelopes for marketing material. I interviewed an employee on the phone after receiving a handwritten invitation to participate in a travel opportunity.

"So, did somebody really handwrite this envelope?" I asked. He explained that his company's statistics for "open rates" were enormously high. "We know that we're going to get someone to open that letter because it was addressed to them personally," he explained. "So, the days of massive email blasts are over?" I questioned. He explained that for their company, this method has been remarkably effective.

Email

Writing to one person directly, through the use of technology, is an acceptable form of business communication. In many circles, it's the only acceptable way businesses and professionals will take in information. Email is a useful tool when materials and data require documented exchanges and for storing data and contact information. For many tasks, email still plays an important role in our 21st-century communication. Until further notice, young adults going into a business setting should still be using email to correspond with colleagues.

There can be a one-to-one nature in email when it's written to just one person. There is a level of feeling that "this is between you and me." However, many businesses, schools, and corporations have policies of "content ownership." Although you may feel like an email is "between you and me," you might be surprised to learn that it's not. Even from your own computer or your smartphone, you have to be mindful that in the digital age of documented data, one click can trigger an irrevocable mistake. And any digital communication that has the ability to reach the world must be constructed with that in mind.

Group email falls under the one-to-many model. It's less personal than the one-to-one models. However, because the senders and receivers of group emails can often see who else is receiving the same information, there is a sense of being part of a team. So, for work or different organizational tasks, email is efficient. It's just important to be mindful of the content. If you have a message that's *expected* to be received personally, for the sake of the relationship, make some calls.

Texting

Texting, as I've been talking about throughout the book, was never intended to become a primary form of communication. I honestly believe that the explosion of our texting culture was a shock for the inventors. It was supposed to be an alternative to a quick note, yet the human factor altered the intention. Where to place "texting" on the most to least personal spectrum created the mostly lively debates among my students. Some of my students who were attached to the texting behavior were visibly emotional and defensive in the debate, and others, who were sick of friends and family members who are nonstop "texters," seemed to be fed up with the behavior.

Despite the different perspectives, we were able to reach the consensus that texting does not feel personal. "As much as I text," said one girl, "I know it's not really personal. I mean, I know you can't really hear how someone is saying something, and I know I am misunderstood all the time."

"Nooooo Jones, not you!"

My friends know I don't like to text. If I do text, I still do it in a way that sounds like a personal letter, saying "Hi" first and usually signing my name at the end. Friends who have received these texts from me, especially those from high school, just laugh. However, I was still trying to embrace the texting world when I remembered I had to tell my friend Judi something. I thought this might be a good use of texting. It was just a short message, and Judi would receive the message at some point during her day.

So, I put my thumbs to work and hit send. A short while later, my phone rang and it was Judi. "I got your message," she said with a pretty straight tone. "I have to tell you, it made me kinda sad." "Oh my God" I thought, "did I screw something up?" She went on to explain, "All I thought was, noooooo Jones, not you...you're the one I get the calls from." Judi continued to explain, "I'm saying to myself, she's writing this book all about technology and communication, and now she's texting. I gotta say it again, it really made me sad!" What I found interesting was that when I was composing the text message, I didn't feel right, or personal. However, I was doing it with a curious sense of the process. I thought to myself, it must be an age thing.

I told that story during a class and was surprised that so many *students agreed* that it didn't feel personal and that yes, when you read a text, it just sounds and feels cold. "But why have we come to embrace such a communication practice?" I wanted to know. "Because it's easy," one student said. Another student chimed in with, "Because we can, and we just got into the habit." Through those discussions, it was apparent that even those who text on a regular basis still agreed that it was not a personal way of connecting.

Journal Entry from Ben

"I wish I had never taught my mother how to text. She will text me all day long. One time, I was so mad at her, because we were all waiting to hear about what colleges my brother got into, and I'm waiting for her to call me, and then, all I got on a text was the name of the college. I was so pissed, I was like, you couldn't call me with this! I mean, it was just so...I don't know, I mean, if you can't depend on your mother [to get a call] for that kind of really important stuff, that's pretty sad."

Just because texting has become ubiquitous in our world doesn't mean that it's appropriate. Texting should be used the way it was intended to be used: if it's something you would say on a "post-it" note — anything from a love note to a phone number, or as a helpful reminder — and used in a limited way, texting can be a useful tool.

Social Media — Restricted

Just by the definition of "social," as in relating to society and the interaction of people, social media was theoretically intended to be people communicating as part of a group. However, depending on the settings you have and how many people are included in that group, you can feel like part of a community or part of the world audience. It can connect like-minded people to specific groups for digital interaction.

Social media, as evaluated on this personal to impersonal spectrum, is not personal simply because of the size of the audience and open access to information. By choosing this medium, you're saying, "This message is for every one of my connections." Even if you're directing your message to one or a few, the medium itself sends the message that this is for lots of eyes and ears. "Lots" is not one or two, or a few. If you're restricting your social media interaction to a limited number of people, where you're allowing access to your information to only a chosen few, it is still considered a form of group communication. It's important to remember that you're communicating in public.

Broadcasting/Social Media — Unrestricted

Social media, blogs, posts, YouTube, Internet channels, and Internet communication are efficient for disseminating information with incredible speed to millions of people. When television ruled, with its ability to reach the masses, the messages were one way. Because of the interactive capabilities of Internet technology, now every person has the power to reach a mass audience, unrestricted. This is 21st-century broadcasting in every sense of the word.

Unrestricted Internet communication, intended to reach the largest audiences possible, obviously cannot be considered personal, although it can feel like that because of the ability for immediate responses from your audience. It's important to be mindful that unrestricted social media and anything that goes through the Internet is public communication. What is written, posted, blogged, or tweeted, unless legally protected, is no longer in your control.

THE SIMPLE SPOON

We all need love, affection and intimacy. Because they are such strong human needs and they can be so complex, we will continue to come up with theories and strategies and books and apps and dating sites, therapy, workshops, and spiritual awakenings, all in the effort to enhance our personal abilities to get the love we want and need. This human behavior is a continuum that will remain a part of the human experience.

Recently, I was reading an interview with a chef. He was asked about his favorite kitchen equipment; he had every gadget, high-end blender, and mixer imaginable. He said he tried everything new that promises easier and more efficient ways to do his job. And yet, his answer to the question, "What is your favorite tool?" was *the spoon*. The spoon is about as old-school as you can get. It's an *ancient* tool from the beginning of civilization. He went on to explain that there is nothing more essential in the cooking process than a really good spoon. Using a really good spoon gave him a good feeling and made him happy.

Really? So simple, right? When something works, and has been working since the beginning of time, it might be worth holding onto and appreciating. Regardless of every new invention and app and gadget, personal remains "personal" and an incredibly vital part of our human experience, despite its simplicity. So many areas of life come back to simple basics.

What we know now, based on years of people trying to figure out how to use our new devices in order to meet our human communication needs, is that we have to admit that at the core of all people is the need for attention, understanding, compassion, empathy, and that feeling of being important to those around us. As impressive as our digital tools can be, and as much as we enjoy them and want to use them, when it comes to our personal connections, our awesome digital devices are leaving us feeling cold. We never seem to really want to admit that.

Chapter 12

Empowerment

"Excellent...Most Righteous...Dude, So-crates"
Bill and Ted's Excellent Adventure

Like a chef who gets the most joy out of an ancient tool like a simple spoon, maybe it's time for us to value the simple things. Maybe instead of a thousand "friends," we'd actually be *happier* with a few "most excellent" ones; instead of obsessively documenting every action of our lives, maybe we'd find more joy in just living in the moment; instead of checking our phones every few minutes, we'd find it more fulfilling to look into the eyes of someone we love. Maybe a momentary warm embrace is better than the constant swipe of a screen.

It's hard to face the fact that life can be tough, as our authentically human experience opens us up to enormous challenges in our emotional, relational, and personal developments. It makes perfect sense for us to look to technology to abolish the growing pains of our experiences and to diminish any inevitable heartache and fear. The truth is that as we spend more time with any screen that is separating us from the authenticity of our raw human interactions, we continue to diminish the actual human experience and the growth potential of intimacy, character, sensitivity, empathy, understanding, patience, and fulfillment. The one thing I hear over and over during my conversations is that *now* is the time to reevaluate our priorities within our daily social interactions.

Is the digitized world meeting the objective of making us more social, more fulfilled, and happier? And if not, then why are we moving toward becoming *more* digitized?

Maybe being authentically human is actually better than *Being Digital.* Nicholas Negroponte's book explains the work going on now at MIT, where digital engineer Gordon Bell focuses on digital storage technology, including the storage of your life memories, as the "inevitable future." As Bell says on his website, "Can you imagine your grandchildren being able to see your life?"

Personally, I'd hope my grandchildren would be focused on the joy and happiness of their own lives. That's just my maternal instinct. But it's important to ask questions. Is this a case of ego-driven immortality? How exactly does that piece of technology align with our values of the human experience? How will this digital hoarding affect and shape us? Why *do* we have to digitally hold on to every memory? Even if we put all that stuff "in a cloud," we're still just collecting more stuff. Isn't the ending to every *Hoarders* television episode about the discovery of some huge hurt in the hoarder's heart?

> "All men's souls are immortal, but the souls of the righteous are immortal and divine."
> — Socrates

If we're living our lives in order to document them, is that in fact actually *living*? That *has* to alter the actual meaning of life. If we're living our lives today for historical preservation, then doesn't that become the purpose of our lives and affect our daily choices? Shouldn't we be focusing on the one life we have right now, and appreciating and experiencing those little moments that end up being an entire life?

We seem to share a general consensus as to what we all want out of life. However, there seems to be a lack of nurturing and valuing the behavior that supports everything we know about happiness. Our happiness comes from our personal accomplishments, our mental and physical well-being and our relationships. Yet we have cultivated a world where isolating ourselves from daily authentic human interaction is more acceptable then ever before. We continue to believe that digital interactions and "social" media are equivalent to, or even an improvement over, traditional interactions. They are *not* the same. The power of authentic human connection has always been a critical component within the human experience. How is it that a couple of decades in the digital world have allowed us to forget that?

"To touch can be to give life."
— Michelangelo

New York writer Diana Spechler, like many professionals these days, works out of her home — a luxury of our digital world. As a result, though, Spechler found herself with less and less human interaction on a daily basis. She was curious whether one could actually be "touch deprived." The answer was Yes.

As we have sadly learned from research decades ago, infants who lack physical human touch, die. Research has shown that physical human interaction, from a casual brushing by of a stranger to hours of cuddling on a couch, provides physical and mental benefits, including reduced stress, anxiety, depression, high blood pressure, and aggression, and increased self-esteem, particularly for adolescents. So maybe we should just ignore the teenage "I'm too cool for hugs" attitude and hug them anyway.

There are enormous physical and mental benefits in touching. Spechler decided to do her own social science experiment for an article in *Oprah* magazine and spent one week incorporating more touching moments in her life whenever she could. For example, Spechler gave a simple little wrist squeeze to a woman as she apologized for stepping on her shoe and gave a friend a much-needed hug. As Spechler found out, "That extra physical connection...a simple action...had conveyed deep meaning." She explained that by the end of the week she was "touching friends, strangers, and coworkers more naturally, and all the contact was making me smile...every touch felt like a little gift to the other person and to me."

The exponential growth of our digital world has been amazing in many ways; however, I have yet to see a corresponding growth in our personal happiness and, more importantly, in meeting the objective of enriching our feelings of connection. What we are actually seeing is the opposite. If, as we get closer to *Being Digital*, which Negroponte says is inevitable, the less happy we are, why would we continue moving in that direction? Isn't *that* a logical question to ask?

EMPOWERMENT

Maybe we'd like to choose happiness instead and focus on our here and now. As I mentioned at the beginning of the book, during the past six years I have been interviewing, listening, and working on a solution to the communication issues and problems that have been unfolding as rapidly as technology has been escalating. My goal has always been to establish some type of protocol that works within the digital world so that we can continue to participate in it, yet to be empowered to opt out of what doesn't feel authentic. The younger generation, without a frame of reference for any other way of life, is being forced to live a life that doesn't feel "right" on some level, yet they have no idea what to do about it. As one high school sophomore explained to me, "It's not really a force, it's more like a perpetual motion thing that grabs onto you, or like a hall of mirrors that you can't escape from." Why are we so afraid to reject new pieces of technology that enter our lives and that we know in our gut aren't serving us well?

On a *Good Morning America* segment in April 2013, the anchors were talking about a new Instagram teen beauty pageant phone app. As Lara Spencer and Josh Elliot were teasing the upcoming story, they were physically cringing at the concept of young girls posting their sexy pictures in order to get "likes" and "win," while other girls were receiving a big red X through their faces when not being chosen.

The news coverage of this story had a group of girls talking about how hurtful this behavior was to their self-esteem. Yet, with all our issues with cyber-bullying, teen depression, and anxiety, why do we continue to allow young kids to have access to this level of negative behavior? Some people, particularly adolescents, simply might not be developmentally ready to handle the responsibilities and the level of power that go along with being able to broadcast every thought to millions. How about asking the question, "When did we decide that a 10-year-old has a right or the emotional maturity to broadcast to the masses?" Because they are children, isn't it our jobs as parents to implement restrictions and simply say certain things are off limits?

What *specific* benefits outweigh what we now know are the negative health risks? Have we actually done the pros and cons list as we blindly accepted this new behavior? In a class conversation, I asked students (a total of 75 from several classes) to do a *pros* and *cons* lists for young kids or adolescents to have their smartphone.

The only thing that students could come up with for the "pros" was that parents were afraid that their child "won't be popular," "won't fit in," or that "they want to make sure their kids are 'cool' and they're a 'cool parent'" and "it's just because it's what every one else has, it's what all the kids are doing," and that was about it. The majority of responses, from those in the 18- to 24-year-old demographic, mind you, were that giving a 10-year-old a smartphone is "just ridiculous."

In the Instagram example, we have to remember that the online pageant wasn't damaging only to the girls who participated, but it also continues to cultivate a level of insensitivity and lack of empathy from participants who found it easy to insult anyone from behind a screen. If the 2010 research shows that the Millennials have seen a reduction in empathetic ability by 40 percent, what might that mean for the next report in 2020 if we continue on this trajectory? Can our culture really afford a world of people who are less caring about one another?

WHAT DO THE KIDS WANT?

What about if we actually listen to what the iGeneration wants? They might be screaming for the next iPhone5C or Samsung Galaxy smartphone because it's a way to impress their friends, but when you really ask them what they want, you might be surprised. The ironic thing is that even though high school and college age students are texting, tweeting, and posting as part of their social communication, they actually *don't like* it, they know it's wrong, and they wish that things were different. In an informal survey in a high school semantics class, students were asked to answer questions on how they communicate in the 21st century. Most of the questions were multiple choice, with the last one being an open response to the question, "If I had a magic wand and could change one thing about the way people communicate with one another today, I would ____." 83.7% responded with some variation of wanting more face-to-face communication and less technology.

> *Of 126 high school students between the ages of 14 and 18, 54 females said they'd like a change, including more face-to-face communication; 7 had no need for change. 49 male students said they'd like a change, including more face-to-face communication; 16 felt no need for any changes.*

FROM THE MOUTHS OF BABES

Having the students handwrite their responses allowed them to be more connected to their feelings. On the same note, *reading* the responses in this form elicits an emotional impact beyond just the statistics. The surprising results were that the majority of those surveyed felt that we need to focus more on one another than on our devices. Here are just some of the comments:

People should communicate face-to-face more than through technology...I would get rid of phones and have only face-to-face conversations...how people rely on phones to feel more comfortable talking b/c it's not in person...how people have little to no communication skills when it comes to face-to-face interactions b/c they are always using cell phones...I would like to see us having more face-to-face conversations...we usually text and I don't like not being able to hear their voice or hear how they are saying something...I would change the social media and text to face-to-face conversations...more face-to-face interaction because it is slowly slipping away...probably more communication at [the] dinner table because we don't have as much these days...use our phones less when we are talking or all hanging out...more face-to-face communication and not having to rely on texting/social media to talk to each other...more face-to-face, not as much texting and tweeting...I would like to change how much we use our phones and how [we] rely on them...have people talk face-to-face more because everyone is too absorbed with their technology...I would take away texting all together and replace it with face-to-face or phone conversation...less social media and more face-to-face...delete Facebook...no texting or instant messaging of any kind...I would make it so that major issues and emotional topics only get communicated face-to-face or in a private phone conversations, as opposed to the increasing trend of everyone weighing in on certain topics [social media]...get rid of cell phones and go back to home land line phones...kill Facebook and make EVERYONE more comfortable talking face-to-face...I would like to see people care about me at least a little...not texting while in the middle of a face-to-face conversation — twitter/Facebook is not your journal…I would like to talk to my mom when she doesn't have her face buried in a phone and completely ignore me — cell phones shouldn't exist…if I could change anything it would be communicating in person, together…I'd get rid of texting, I feel like we'd all be a little more social and "human" if we just called each other instead of texting…I would have better communication skills with my family.

Again, these are the words of *young people* between the ages of 14 and 18. It seems so obvious that they're looking for a way out of this cycle. We continue to deal with increasing issues of cyber-bullying, depression, anxiety, stress, and a host of other concerns, so why aren't we listening to our children? Granted, we know that these kids who are saying we need more face-to-face conversations are the same kids who would need a linebacker to wrestle the phone *out* of their hand. However, doesn't it sound as though there would be a sense of *relief* if that magic wand wiped away the demands of 24/7 digital connections? This is where we need to work together.

CHANGES

"And these children that you spit on…they're quite aware of what they're going through."
— David Bowie

A group of students who were deeply motivated by the conversations, lessons, and experiments during our classes together continued to keep in touch with me as they've considered these questions and engaged in debates with their own friends. Since ending our official classes together, they continued to practice some of the authentic communication principles that empowered them to make personal changes to the way they connect in our digital world.

For over a year, as each student focused on building their own human communication apps, they continued to feel happier and less stressed overall, and they encouraged their own friends and family members, including those of the iGeneration, to join them in participating in a greater life-to-technology ratio.

"Downgrading my phone has upgraded my life."
— Ben, Emerson College

There is no way it is humanly possible to keep up with every new digital communication trend. It is maddening to even try. We just have to know that as Facebook use is declining and Twitter and Instagram or SnapChat may be the way to go, for now anyway, in six months something else will take over. As apps come and go, the one thing that will remain constant is the authentic communication needs of the human being.

What we cannot dispute, and what we have known about mankind for thousands of years, is that our connections with others are rooted in authenticity. When our focus is on developing our most genuine human communication and social skills, with the clear understanding of our own needs and the needs of others, the digital tools of the moment will be irrelevant. As we become more personally empowered, we'll be able to see our devices as just tools...*not your lifeline.*

ONE WEEK TO ONE YEAR

"Oh my God, that's right, it was exactly one year ago that we did the digital cleanse," Billi said as we met up. Ben jumped in to remind us that he was really responsible for the Billi and Steve love connection, saying "Remember, I was the one who said we were all gonna meet at the bar and since we were all doing the cleanse together, you and Steve hung out socially for the first time?" Billi continued, "Yeah, because I was freaking out that I was just starting the digital cleanse on St. Patrick's

Day...in Boston...and I wasn't going to have my phone with me!"

The first thing Billi said when she showed up for the first class after their weekend without phones was, "Thank God I didn't have my phone on me...no drunk texting or worrying about my phone!" I said, "So, over this whole year, you guys really stayed with the system and never really went back to the way you used to use your technology, is that right?" Ben explained, "Well, you just feel so much better, I mean the other way just doesn't feel organic."

"Oh, everything is really good...I have a beautiful girlfriend, I feel good," Steve said. "I mean, I still have a Facebook page, but honestly, we hardly ever use it." Billi added, "Unless someone from the family in Italy is sending me stuff and I get an email notification from someone to go to their page, but I don't go on it at all on a regular basis or feel like I have to post anything."

Ben chimed in with, "I totally deactivated my Facebook account and downgraded my phone, and I'm so much happier and my relationships are so much better. You can't believe the reaction that you get when people say, 'Can I friend you on Facebook?' and I say, 'I'm not on Facebook.' They're really intrigued and want to know why and I get into really interesting conversations about the fact that being on Facebook just really makes you feel like shit. You don't feel better, you just feel worse. It's so funny because everyone agrees and then I [really] feel better."

I asked him to explain what he meant by feeling better. "Would you say empowered?" I asked. "Yeah, exactly, empowered because you really don't need it," he said. I was mostly curious to see if this system could actually be sustainable for this generation, so I asked them, "Would you guys say that you could opt out if you want?"

"Absolutely," Billi explained. "Stephen and I had such a great trip to Europe and we were just focused on ourselves and enjoying the trip. Instead of technology we brought our cribbage game and we were drinking wine and playing on the train to Amsterdam. But, the other thing was that we never felt compelled to have to post our pictures or say 'Hey everyone, look at us, we're on the train, or we're eating now...or whatever.' We actually enjoyed each other and the trip and didn't have that feeling of having to share it with anyone else. I mean we took pictures and will show everyone...but we weren't taking pictures for [the purpose of] posting."

Because I'm publishing this communication system for the digital age, I asked, "What would you say really worked for you most?" Ben replied, "Well, I'd have to say it really started with understanding the actual communication process and what people are all about...I mean, what we really need. The biggest lesson for me was the empathetic listening. I can't tell you how now so many of my friends will call me, because I'll listen to them." "And...that's a good thing?" I asked, laughing. Ben explained, "Yeah, I know, right...but also, knowing that it's important. I mean, I have friends that will text me over and over and I'll just pick up the phone and call them and I won't text them back until they pick up the phone and call me. I have a friend who can get thousands of hits on a YouTube site, but can't pick up the phone and talk to me."

"What about the cleanse?" I asked. "Is this something that people have to do?" Unanimous decision: "Oh absolutely." All three commented, "You have to do the cleanse to get the perspective...and, to get out of the 'bubble'...you won't know what it's like until you really experience it...and to see how all the people around you react...and to see really how addicted you are to your phone. The digital cleanse is the real eye-opener part, then you can do the steps."

TRENDING: AUTHENTICITY

All over the Internet and news shows there are stories of people doing some version of our digital cleanse. A *Today Show* report by anchor Natalie Morales followed a group of girls who locked their phones away in a suitcase to see if they could go on a digital diet for a week. They revealed the same feelings as many of my students, reporting that they felt "free, less stressed, less anxious, more focused," and that overall their relationships were closer and their communication with their close friends felt more fulfilling. However, without the reeducation and a plan, all of those interviewed just went back to their old habits.

Even the most ardent techies are realizing they're getting lost in the obsessiveness of their own passion. Interestingly, even those whom we considered the ultimate *techies* simply "felt better" with less technology.

Google design partner Jake Knapp tried his version of a digital cleanse for a week and admitted to feeling much better, saying he "can't handle infinity in his pocket." Knapp wrote about his experience on the gadget website *Gizmodo*, saying that being bored can be a good thing and can allow some of those "sweet" moments of life to be experienced. Or, as Ben said in his email to me suggesting that I read the article, "You just freakin' feel better." Of course, he reminded me that this class started the trend two years ago! Knapp's self-proclaimed hypocrisy relates to so many with a love/hate relationship with their devices, saying, "It's not that I don't enjoy the iPhone, it's just that I only want half of it."

THE EVOLUTION OF THE DIGITAL REBELS

The digital pull of our society deliberately makes it hard to opt out completely, since this is the world we live in. One 16-year-old high school student, who grew up without social media use in his home, was naturally curious about it and also interested in seeing why some school clubs that he belonged to only used Facebook to communicate.

He wasn't interested in having a personal Facebook page, because he knew of all the "drama" his friends were going through. However, since he didn't want to keep bothering people for the information about club meetings, he got a Facebook page under a false name. "In a way it was good for me to have the experience first hand, because now I know how it feels. Within the first three days I got that sick feeling," he explained, adding that he was exposed to stuff he wished he hadn't seen.

"I always heard my friends talking about those feelings, but now I can talk from experience. I can tell you, it totally sucks." As a teen new to the consequences of social media's "sucker punch" and "Russian roulette" communication, what he found even more bizarre was the voyeuristic component. He explained, "It was almost like looking through the windows of people's lives. I mean, you would never walk up to someone's house and look at them through their window, but that's sort of what it felt like. I didn't like it."

It's not easy to go against the norm. This is not simply swimming upstream. For many, this is trying to catch a breath of air from beneath a tidal wave. And for those who don't know any other way, the thought of leaving something so familiar, whether it's good or bad, is hard to even contemplate.

The qualities that got us hooked on social media are the same qualities that prevent us from being able to escape. By our nature, we are creatures of curiosity, ego, fear, and attention that sometimes (or often) work against our intellectual judgment. As humans, our actions are almost always driven by our feelings. If we're curious, we want to feed that curiosity with answers. We get an ego boost from seeing our own images. We feel like we have some control constructing a digital life that represents what *we'd like* it to be. We want people to be able to find us. How can we move beyond the pull of this digitally demanding world?

"I get by with a little help from my friends."
— Lennon/McCartney (the last hit song they wrote together)

THE REBEL ALLIANCE

The common denominator for anyone who has actually transformed their lives is that they have reached the point where they can honestly say, "This isn't working for me." Many people are now coming to realize that their relationships with their devices and social media sites, even though they're considered today's "social norm," are having a negative effect on their mental and emotional well-being. Some are now seeking treatment for addiction, anxiety, and stress related to dependency on their devices, as we see "digital detox" camps becoming the rage for those who can afford that luxury. Others are making smaller changes in their daily behavior. Either way, the one thing that everyone needs to know is that you *do* have a choice.

"Facebook is like (the movie) *Mean Girls* times like five million."
— Billi, Fashion Retail Management, NEiA

For these students, breaking the habit of the nonstop connectivity, practicing the mindful communication method to "step up" to more personal connections whenever possible, and removing themselves from the negativity and "obligation" of social media made them feel better and more fulfilled. It was those feelings that they shared with their friends and family.

"It just starts like **this**," Billi explained. "I just told my best friend that this isn't working for me, so if you need me, just call me. And, then *she* ended up getting off of Facebook too." Steve added, "I never liked it to begin with. I always preferred being able to just talk to people." And Ben followed, "I got my sister to do it and a few friends, and I think maybe because they didn't have the whole class to learn all the other stuff, they couldn't stick with it. But I'd say they definitely got it. They definitely understand what I was talking about.

"What are you going to do with your one and only life?"
— Viola Davis in *Won't Back Down*

For some, it seems like they need permission to leave. When they hear that other people have been feeling the same way, and hear that others have made the choice to "opt-out" and are not only doing just fine but are actually happier, it's easier to join the exodus. I mentioned one student, Brendon, who decided to delete his Facebook account as we were having an after-class conversation, and I was curious about why exactly he was able to make that decision.

During a follow-up interview, he explained that the class conversations were motivating but also that he "spent a lot of time thinking about deleting Facebook because I just didn't feel the need to have my whole life up there. It gave me a weird anxiety, always getting tagged in pictures, no matter where I went. It took away from the life experience I wanted." He continued, saying to me "You brought up the point that if everyone feels this way, then why isn't everyone stopping the behavior, so I decided right then and there [to delete his page]. I mean I sit here whining about it so why would I go home and get on Facebook afterward?"

The conversation that I had with Brendon is representative of the many one-to-one conversations I have had with my students, when given the opportunity to dig a little deeper than the superficially-generated comments of a digitally-connected life. "Everyone feels the same way, they complain but always have reasons why they won't get rid of it," he continued. "But, it's not an easy thing to do, is it?" I asked. He explained that it's mostly about "fear, losing access to invitations, but the cons outweigh the pros. [Facebook] consistently forces you to compare yourself to everyone else. It's a competition...a sense of loneliness...a highway to everyone else's life. It's an insane way to go through life. It doesn't make you feel good at all."

"You cannot protect yourself from sadness without protecting
yourself from happiness."
— Jonathan Safran Foer

Brendon concluded that when he deleted his Facebook page, it inspired his girlfriend to do the same. And as he explained, "I like life better...I know the word 'free' is cliché to say, but it's true."

Ben reported why he got off all social media, saying that "Part of that stress for me when you're on those sites was the competitiveness. You have to have the most comments...most likes, and you have to keep checking [for updates]." He described to me a time when his friend posted something and then kept checking and checking for hours, finally turning to Ben and saying, "Now I feel like shit because I didn't get more than five likes." I asked Billi, Ben, and Steve why they were able to opt out of the social media and smartphone habits. Ben replied, "We just realized it was not organic." Billi added, "It's not going to lead to anything...it's just a mess of people and you really can't even connect with anyone...it's just cluttering your mind, it blocks you and fogs you...with drama...it's a fog machine."

It seems that our intrinsic human nature is demanding more of those simple but more fulfilling moments of our lives. Brendon remembered, "When me and my friends used to be in the car together, we'd be laughing and talking, and now it's just quiet, everyone looking down at their phones." People are admittedly feeling less connected and want a change. Brendon continued, "I think we have to reevaluate at this point...stop and realize that it is not good for us to live our lives with this constant competition. We all agree it's messing with people's heads."

LOL

"There's nothing like deep breaths after laughing that hard. Nothing in the world like a sore stomach for the right reasons." — Stephen Chbosky, *The Perks of Being a Wallflower*

For the purpose of choosing happiness, LOL is about **Living Off Line**. One of the secrets to happiness is living a life that is most authentically you, which unfolds through your authentic relationships. I was curious about how it is to live life in the digital age when you set clear boundaries in this time of 24/7 nonstop connections. Steve explained that his self-esteem is so much better. "I've grown...Facebook and texting used to bring me down. Now I just live a life [with my] beautiful girlfriend [and] less stress." Billi added, "Downgrading sparks a little excitement from others. It's a good model because you're more individualistic. You feel like more people are flocking *to* you. You're happier and a viable charismatic source of life." And Ben said, "It's like a virus. I was living a life that was half awake. You're only half yourself." He joked, "That's why I watch reality TV...when I want to turn off half my brain!"

When we work on our own personal development, acquire greater self-esteem and confidence, and feel comfortable in our own skin, the laws of attraction work for us, and we begin to actually experience those fulfilling connections that we try in vain to receive by spending hours on the Internet.

Choosing the quick fix has always been part of our human nature. From the invention of the wheel to our smartphones, it's easy to see why we look outside ourselves for "advancement." What we forget to do is appreciate the fact that we are *more* amazing than any piece of technology. Our fulfillment and pride in ourselves comes from challenging our potential. Perhaps it's the fear of acknowledging our own limitations that prevents us from even attempting to do things that challenge us. While some techies are focused on all the things that gadgets can do for us, like the "memory storage" technology on the horizon, others dare to challenge the authentic capacity of their own minds.

Joshua Foer's book *Moonwalking with Einstein: The Art and Science of Remembering Everything* chronicles the writer's achievements as a mental athlete whose training made him the winner of the U.S Memory Championship. We might not all be able to memorize the pattern of a deck of cards in a minute, but there is a wonderful philosophy that the secret to life and to our deepest joy lies within the process of self-mastery. In other words, it's not necessarily the accomplishment itself, but working on the *process* of becoming our personal best that leads to greater satisfaction. And, in the biggest trick of life's crazy game, our personal enlightenment is achieved when we can accept and then find contentment with our unfolding self-discoveries of our authentic selves.

Human evolution isn't about creating technology that can think for us, connect for us, do for us. Our evolution is about how we can evolve our own thinking and turn our knowledge into wisdom. It's about how we can do better for ourselves and for one another. This is the oldest universal lesson and it's one that for some reason we have lost sight of. Our success and our happiness is a choice and lies within ourselves. It is not in the new iPhone and it cannot be Googled.

"What's interesting," Steve reminded us, "is that the CEO of Google didn't become the CEO of Google by Googling it. He had to use his brain. He had to go out there and live life and learn."

"So, what do you want to do to change the world?" I asked these students who are in charge of the future. "Do you feel that an authentic life experience cannot be experienced through our mediated, digital world and that people are now coming to that point of realization?" Billi explained that so many people don't even know why they're not feeling good. "You have to remove yourself...you need to say, all this over connecting is not good for me, so, I'm not doing it. The revolution [starts] in your mind."

It's time to look at the culture that we are creating and ask the questions about how our mediated world is contributing to the condition our society is in. We need to think about the trajectory we are on now, so that we can, perhaps for the first time, actually learn from history and change our course.

We have a long history of ignoring the signs until it's too late. What actually has to happen for a society to shift its values?

THE FASTEST SOLUTION

"It only takes a few to start an epidemic."
— Malcolm Gladwell, *The Tipping Point*

In *The Tipping Point*, Malcolm Gladwell states that it only takes a few people to start a revolution. "Ideas are catching," as the author explains on his website. This is why **you** are so important. A new trend can change the world overnight. You are the trendsetters. As one student said, "Why is it always us? You guys (I'm assuming he was referring to the fact that I am older than 30) are the ones that screwed it up for us."

"Well, actually," I responded, "it's always someone of your generation who has had the power to influence the world. Think about it, from Marconi and Farnsworth, who invented the radio and television, to Zuckerberg and Jobs, they were all in the 18- to 25-year-old demographic when they made their communication contributions to the world." So, *your* legacy, you 18- to 25-year-olds, may be returning authenticity to the human experience.

POSITIVE EPIDEMICS

We have the makings of a positive social epidemic — a small group of young people who are experiencing changes in their lives and who have the courage, strength, confidence, communication, and leadership skills to model a different type of behavior that is beginning to spread.

When I asked, "So what do you want to do?" Billi explained, speaking on behalf of the group, "We want to set an example to show that the world still revolves when you're not on Facebook, or when your phone dies...no one freaks out. Look, we set a time and plan to be here and we're here." Billi was referring to the fact that Ben had left his phone charger in Florida on spring break so he didn't have a phone. Billi and Steve showed up an hour earlier than planned, but we had made a plan, with a date and time — we didn't confirm and text a million times, we just *trusted* that we'd all be together. And we were.

What if being connected 24/7 is not the cool thing to do any more? You are the trendsetters. If you want to see things change quickly, and save the next generation from the problems that you've been going through, then do as Gandhi said. *"Be the change you want to see."* You actually can downgrade your phone, get off social media, and build your personal confidence by being the one who can take it or leave it. Be the one *in control*. No pressure. Your future is really up to you.

The truth is, if you're looking to change things and you're depending on the grownups, it will never happen fast enough for you to benefit. The older generation and the stockholders on Wall Street will start the same spin as they did for all the other corporately-engineered addictions, like sugar or tobacco. They will spend the next decade doing research and producing studies that will contradict anything that threatens the bottom line of their corporation. The only way the digital takeover might subside is when those select few — the most popular kids in school, a few rock stars, or a major movie star with enough self-esteem who can actually *model* the behavior and decide not to be a tool — actually make the change. Then others will follow.

Technology has its place, just not in our psyche. We encourage those with the talent and genius to create technology to clean up our environment, protect the ozone, cure cancer, heal the wounded...those are all wonderful places for technical advances. Don't mess with what makes us human. Stop deceptive media messages that use emotion-based words to try to convince us that love, fulfillment, emotional connections, and human happiness can be created with a new app. Keep technology out of our spirit, our emotions, our self-esteem, our relationships, our emotional intelligence, our vulnerability toward fear, obsession, addiction, and our patience with one another.

FINAL THOUGHTS

It's hard to embrace the paradox of good and bad at the same time. For over a decade now, we have been witness to the worst and best in our humanity. Our humanity is all that we've got...that and each other. From 9/11 to the Newtown school shootings and the Boston Marathon bombing, the root of both the damage and the healing is ultimately in the souls of our humanity.

Whenever we really need to feel emotionally connected, we find a way to touch each other. Our technology can keep us informed like never before. However, the healing is in the hands. During the Newtown shooting tragedy, thousands showed up to stand shoulder to shoulder, teary wet cheek to teary wet cheek. After the Boston bombing, people through-out the Boston area were holed up in their homes for 24 hours, receiving information and watching the manhunt un-fold in real time through technology. Yet, the moment it was over, thousands and thousands felt the need to run out into the streets to touch and hug and stand *Boston Strong* in ap-preciation of the work done by the authorities. We witnessed an unprecedented example of egos and money being put on the back burner, as the focus was on the one goal of saving lives.

As we witnessed the best in humanity, we also wit-nessed the worst. The human ego and social media don't necessarily make a good combination. It was sad to see many people spreading rumors and jokes, and showing a level of insensitivity in regard to graphic pictures that would have been considered the ultimate invasion of privacy and respect only a few years ago. The question remains, what parts of our humanity do we want to cultivate?

The truth is that we have gotten off track in our connec-tion industry, and it is obvious we need to make a correction. The challenge will be whether we can find enough people who are brave enough to admit it and start making those corrections.

I believe that before we teach our children how to talk to a *million* people in a fraction of a second, we should first teach them how to talk to just *one.* Before we allow them to tune into the static sounds of our mediated world, we should teach them how to tune into the quiet whisper of their own reflective thoughts. Instead of working on your *brand,* work on *yourself.* Incorporate the *Embrace and Let Go* paradox of embracing the good in technology and knowing how to let go for greater personal fulfillment. Implement boundaries for your own sanity and restrictions for your children if you real-ly want them to experience a life free of digital demands and the threats of public humiliation.

As I said in the beginning of the book, I am an idealist. However, I have seen the reality of change and accomplishment when we put ego aside and work together. We can shape a better world for you, your friends, your family, and all of humanity when we do things in the spirit of sharing our human experience. We have to accept that no piece of technology, no digital device, and no app will ever come close to giving us the soul-to-soul connection that we can only receive from one another. And why would we want it any other way?

Appendix

Solution Box

Since I have been working on this project, all I hear is the resignation in my students' voices as they say, "What can you do?" The feeling of total helplessness in the face of today's social media onslaught is palpable. The first step in overcoming these feelings is to start by making small changes in your own life. This will create a ripple effect, first among those closest to you and then, as they catch on to your positive reactions, throughout your generation. It will start with a personal feeling of empowerment, and then you will be shocked to see how much power you truly have.

Support companies that support people first. In other words, don't bank at companies that make you pay extra in order to speak with a teller.

Tell your parents that they should not allow your younger brothers and sisters to continue to be socialized online.

Facebook and the latest, greatest social media sites are not as cool as they're cracked up to be. Face it, the second that your parents think texting is cool, it's time for you to insist that talking in person is the new thing to do. When you become friends with your dentist on Facebook, it's time to close it down.

Understand that less is more. Focus on your core five or ten friends. If they have your back, you don't need anything else.

Don't spend time being a digital voyeur, living your life looking through a window into the lives of others. It's so much more fulfilling to focus on your own life. Get out there and live an authentic life.

Don't have sex with anyone you can't have a conversation with.

Don't go out with anyone who doesn't have the decency to call you and ask you out on a date. If he or she doesn't have the tact (or the time) to make a phone call or talk to you face-to-face to ask you out, how exciting do you think that first date is going to be, as he or she sits across from you pecking away with his or her thumbs?

Repeat this mantra daily: I am human; I have all the apps I need.

YOUR SUGGESTIONS WELCOME

Here are some of the conversations I've been imagining. Maybe we can put our heads together and collaborate and come up with ways of improving things that we are not happy about.

1 *Dear Corporate America:*

Try the concept of Karma Marketing. In other words, believe that if you focus your energy on doing the right thing, serving in the best interest of your customers, it will all come back to you in greater profits. (Stop laughing!! Somebody out there has to have the guts to try!)

Allow for down time. Do not email your employees 24 hours a day and expect replies at 3:00 A.M. Be a company that values people. You will get the best talent.

Can you image if one corporate giant says our policy is that we believe people need boundaries? So, we're going to give staff members an office with a door to work in private and make calls uninterrupted and without the glare of someone in the next cubicle listening in. And we'll have collaborative meetings together to brainstorm and work off each other's energy. And then (are you ready...) tell your employees to "have a good weekend, ponder and reflect a bit, and we'll check in with each other again on Monday." Your employees are incredibly creative when they're encouraged to "think."

2 *Dear Digital Giants:*

You have made a gazillion dollars from us. You win — we're hooked. So it might be the responsible thing for you to help clean up some of the damage. At one point the tobacco industry had to fund public service announcements about tobacco addiction. How about our technology industries putting some money behind some mediated messages that value our authentic communications.

I've got plenty of campaign slogans ready to roll. I have teams of creative students ready with their cameras, talent, ideas, and original music. We will roll these out for a fraction of what you would pay Madison Avenue ad agencies.

Corporations are looking for employees who have excellent communication skills in addition to technical skills. It would be helpful and beneficial in the long run for you to underwrite education programs in order to properly train our young people with the personal communication skills and lessons in the humanities that produce the well-rounded people you're seeking to employ.

3   *Dear National Association of Broadcasters (NAB) and FCC bigwigs:*

You are missing such an opportunity here. Think James Earl Jones: "If you build it, they will come." We are at the digital saturation point and are desperate for one place to get news and information where the focus is on credibility more than immediacy.

Right now, the only example of honest and ethical news and information is on Aaron Sorkin's HBO series The Newsroom. *When I played a clip from the show that described journalistic integrity, the first comment I heard from a student was "If only…"*

Maybe it's time we put one hour of noncommercial information broadcasting on television without any corporate influence, where news and information have been triple-checked before being broadcast. In other words, "right" not "first." How's this as a slogan: "Here at [news station name], we'd rather be right instead of first."

I'm sure Mr. Sorkin would be thrilled to see his model implemented in real life. You have an opportunity to reply to viewers who "don't know what to believe in anymore." We cannot continue to have legitimate news organizations contributing to the mass distribution of misinformation.

Please stop lowering standards on sex and violence. We have plenty of options on the Internet and subscription channels for people who choose that form of entertainment. Broadcast television might have an opportunity to offer a different option by upholding a set of broadcast standards instead of trying to compete on a content level with the Internet.

4 *Dear Celebrities:*

Have a little class. Let your work speak for itself. Don't be so desperate that you think the only way you will have a public following is if you are tweeting and texting...leave that for the wannabes. Follow the star quality behavior of Emma Watson, George Clooney, Daniel Radcliffe, and Julia Roberts, who don't exude desperation by begging the world to "follow them." Be a celebrity who follows the philosophy, "If you have something to say, say something." Use your public platform for changing and improving humanity.

Model the behavior for privacy so that impressionable young people actually value their own privacy and the privacy of others.

5 *Dear U.S. Department of Education, Colleges, and High School and Grade School Educators:*

We were told that computers and technology were the answer to learning. Check out the cover of Newsweek *circa 1984. It was all about computers being the answer to education. And yet, here we are being referred to as "The Dumbest Generation." Studies have shown that after 20 years of incorporating computers into classrooms, teachers who can inspire and engage students still create the best educational results. Support, reward, and fund teachers who give their hearts and souls to creating a better future for our young people.*

We have great models of education that work. Consider Freeman Hrabowski of the University of Maryland, Baltimore, who uses people to inspire a love of math and science, the two areas where there is the greatest job demand.

And think of Duke University president Richard H. Brodhead, who reminds us that education in the social sciences and humanities has produced "many of the country's most successful and creative people."

Act now. Every primary, middle, and high school needs to decide on a communication philosophy with very specific guidelines. First, there needs to be a clear understanding of what is considered appropriate and inappropriate. Our social norms are changing daily because of technology, so this has to be part of a curriculum. Have students decide on a long list, post it, and have students recognize "inappropriate" behavior as soon as they see it. It is not fair to have students punished for being "inappropriate" when they are exposed to all sorts of "inappropriate" behavior everywhere they go — on social media, at home, at work, and in movies and television. They can only be held accountable for inappropriate behavior when they know in advance what that entails, not with this trial-and-error method that we've been using. If we teach them what is appropriate, we can also teach them to "pay it forward" when they encounter bad behavior at school.

Schools should also adopt policies that allow students the choice to opt out of social media websites. Whether they are officially addictive or not, students should not have to feel like they have to be on Facebook or Twitter in order to be up to speed with their school activities. Because we now know that the nature of using social media can elicit negative behavior and "keyboard courage" comments, schools should not be using profit-making sites such as Facebook for communicating information about clubs, sports, and school-related activities. All school communication should be on school websites.

"School websites are lame," as I was informed. Suggestion: give students the job of running a school website. Post pictures or videos from theater and sporting events to share on a smaller scale, which "reinforces collaboration and community." The benefit is that information, data, and photos remain within the

ownership and control of the students and parents instead of being owned by Mark Zuckerberg or YouTube. The running of a website also offers valuable lessons in entrepreneurship, creativity, and collaboration, which are all skills that are in high demand in the work force.

These are just some suggestions that have come from brainstorming conversations. If you have some good ideas, collaborate with your friends, family, or business associates and try them out.

We're supposed to always be focusing on how we can make things "better." Not faster and easier, but better for us as individuals and as a community.

Thank You

As we've been saying throughout this book, every single person is born with the wiring to be understood. This process begins at birth and is not over until death. How we achieve that remains within our human communication process and our relationships.

Reading someone's written thoughts creates a relationship between writer and reader. I want to thank you for taking the time to listen to my thoughts and feelings on this subject. Whether you agree or disagree, I sincerely appreciate the fact that you've invested the time to listen to me.

In the few weeks before this book went to press I've had more and more people tell me that through our conversations, they've become more aware of their digital life and have come to understand why they have been feeling the way they feel. At the same time Google Glass is getting ready to launch their "wearable computer," I'm finding more people putting their phones away, choosing instead to experience life more authentically. One student explained, "Just since we've been talking about this, I've wanted to try just not holding my phone everywhere I go. I just feel so much better. It's really weird — I didn't think that just putting my phone in my bag would make such a difference, but I actually feel less stressed and happier."

When people talk honestly, one-on-one or in groups, just knowing that someone else feels the way they feel can transform lives. If you'd like to join us to talk about all these issues further, we can be reached through **cellingyoursoul.com** or **NoAppForLife.com.** I wish you the very best, and I look forward to meeting you!

Very special thanks —

*The worst problem I could possibly face is that I have **too** many people to thank. If this were my Oscar speech, the music would be coming up as they'd be dragging me off the stage, desperate not to forget to mention all those beautiful souls who have touched my life in ways that they probably don't even know. So, in the spirit of keeping it short, thank you.*

I'd like to thank all the students who are featured in this book, especially Ben, Billi, and Steve, for graciously sharing your thoughts and your time, for all the conversations and work on this entire project. You are extraordinarily talented and beautiful people who have a wonderful life ahead of you!

My personal appreciation for my son, Morgan. You are an exceptional person who shows enormous empathy, under- standing, and love for all the people in your life. I respect your courage, wisdom, talent, passion, and strength in a world of enormous challenges. Thank you for your patience during this project, and thank you for the ultimate joy in hearing your laughter and for the honor of being your mother.

My thanks to an incredible family: my parents, Louis and Jeanne; my sister Jeannie; and my nieces Katie and Kelly and my nephew Michael. There is a level of love and support for one another that is invaluable and goes beyond what any family could possibly wish for.

I am blessed to have a special person that I simply refer to as my best friend. Together since we were six, our initials carved in cement as J.S. + D.B. 4-ever...we have been. Everyone should have one best friend, and I'm lucky to have the best one in my friend Diane.

Knowing that listening is love, I am tremendously loved by those who have listened to me. As an extrovert, I processed all this information out loud! Thank you to my love Dan for your incredible support, insightful feedback, and patience...my wonderful and beautiful girlfriends, Anne, Paula, Susan, Judi, Valerie, Denni, Joanne, Rose, Betsy and Kitty...your friendship, laughter, love, and loyalty have been a blessing. To my friend and editor Liz — without your help and guidance, this would never have been finished! To Rose, for all her last-minute help. And to Steve, my mentor and friend, for teaching me about the incredible complexities of human beings and guiding me through my own life's journey, my sincere thanks.

I would like to go on...(music has been playing now for a few minutes...)...so, THANK YOU!

Works Cited

"4 in 10 College Kids Are Depressed, Hopeless." *Msnbc.com.* N.p., n.d. Web. 22 July 2013.

"Antidepressant Use Up 400 Percent in US | Psych Central News." *Psych Central.com.* N.p., n.d. Web. 25 Feb. 2013.

Cacioppo, John T. "Epidemic of Loneliness Loneliness Is Far More than a Social Misfortune." *Psychology Today.* N.p. 3 May 2009. Web.

Carr, Nicholas G. *The Shallows: What the Internet Is Doing to Our Brains.* New York: W.W. Norton, 2010. Print.

Centers for Disease Control and Prevention. Centers for Disease Control and Prevention, 10 Apr. 2012. Web. 22 July 2013.

"Children Targets of $1.6 Billion in Food Ads." *Washington Post.* N.p., 30 July 2008. Web. 22 Feb. 2013.

"Classics in the History of Psychology – A.H. Maslow (1943) A Theory of Human Motivation." *Classics in the History of Psychology – A.H. Maslow (1943) A Theory of Human Motivation.* Np., n.d. Web. 20 Oct. 2013.

Collins, Sandra D. "Listening." *Managerial Communication.* Thousand Oaks: Sage, 2001. Print.

Collins, Sandra Dean., and James S. O'Rourke. *Interpersonal Communication: Listening and Responding.* Mason, OH: South-Western Cengage Learning, 2009. Print.

Dokoupil, Tony. "Is the Web Driving Us Mad?" *The Daily Beast.* Newsweek/Daily Beast, 09 July 2012. Web. 25 Feb. 2013.

Dunbar, Robin. "The Social Brain Hypothesis." *Psych.colorado. edu.* N.p., n.d. Web.

"Educator Services Teaching & Learning Curriculum Resources Massachusetts Curriculum Frameworks." *Current Curriculum Frameworks.* N.p., n.d. Web. 20 May 2013.

"Epidemic of Loneliness." *Psychology Today.* N.p., n.d. Web.

"An Estimated 1 in 10 U.S. Adults Report Depression." *Centers for Disease Control and Prevention,* 31 Mar. 2011. Web. 22 July 2013.

Foer, Joshua. *Moonwalking with Einstein: The Art and Science of Remembering Everything.* New York: Penguin, 2011. Print.

Giles, David. *Illusions of Immortality: A Psychology of Fame and Celebrity.* New York: St. Martin's, 2000. Print.

"Gladwell Dot Com - Malcolm Gladwell, Blink, Tipping Point and New Yorker Articles." *Gladwell Dot Com - Malcolm Gladwell, Blink, Tipping Point and New Yorker Articles.* N.p., n.d. Web. 18 Feb. 2013.

Gladwell, Malcolm. *The Tipping Point: How Little Things Can Make a Big Difference.* Boston: Little, Brown, 2000. Print.

Grossman, Lev. "Breaking News, Analysis, Politics, Blogs, News Photos, Video, Tech Reviews." *Time.* Time, Feb. 2011. Web. 18 Mar. 2013.

"Health Risks of Heavy Drinking." *Men's Health Magazine: Men's Guide to Fitness, Health, Weight Loss, Nutrition, Sex, Style and Guy Wisdom.* N.p., n.d. Web. 25 Feb. 2013.

Helliwell, John. "World Happiness Report." *World Happiness Report* (2012). N.p. Web.

"How Facebook Makes Lonely People Even Lonelier" Revealed by Distinguished University of Chicago Professor in Interview with Brian Vaszily on IntenseExperiences. com. N.p., n.d. Web. 05 May 2013.

<Http://www.businessinsider.com/josh-harris-net-band-command-2012-10#ixzz2SumKmhnI.> N.p., n.d. Web.

Human Communication. A Publication of the Pacific and Asian Communication Association. Human Communication. Vol. 12. N.p., n.d. Web.

"Inappropriate Prescribing." *Inappropriate Prescribing.* N.p., n.d. Web. 25 Feb. 2013.

International Journal of Technoethics (IJT). IGI Global: (1947-3451)(1947-346X): *Rocci Luppicini: Journals.* N.p., n.d. Web. 30 Mar. 2013.

Johnson, Clay A. *The Information Diet: A Case for Conscious Consumption.* Sebastopol, CA: O'Reilly Media, 2012. Print.

Kaiser Family Foundation. <http://www.kff.org/entmedia/upload/8010.pdf> N.p., n.d. Web.

Konrath, Sara. "U-M Study: College Students Don't Display as Much Empathy as They Used to." Research at UM RSS. N.p., n.d. Web. 04 Mar. 2013.

Lanier, Jaron. *You Are Not a Gadget: A Manifesto.* New York: Alfred A. Knopf, 2010. Print.

"Lee Siegel on the Perils of Parenting in the Digital Age." *Lee Siegel on the Perils of Parenting in the Digital Age.* N.p., n.d. Web. 20 Oct. 2013.

"Managers to Millennials: Job Interview No Time to Text." *USA Today.* Gannett, n.d. Web. 20 May 2013.

"Media Use by Children Younger Than 2 Years." *Media Use by Children Younger Than 2 Years.* N.p., n.d. Web. 06 July 2013.

"Microstructure Abnormalities in Adolescents with Internet Addiction Disorder." *PLOS ONE.* N.p., n.d. Web. 25 Feb. 2013.

"Millennials Are WAY Too Immature At The Office." *Business Insider Australia.* N.p., n.d. Web. 30 Mar. 2013.

"Millennials: The Next Greatest Generation?" *US Millennials The Next Greatest Generation Comments.* N.p., n.d. Web. 17 July 2013.

"MIT Researchers Aim to Create Nutritional Label for Your News Diet | Poynter." *Poynter.* N.p., n.d. Web. 25 Feb. 2013.

Negroponte, Nicholas. *Being Digital.* New York: Knopf, 1995. Print.

"A Nutrition Label for the News." *WGBH News.* N.p., n.d. Web. 25 Feb. 2013.

"On Leadership." *Washington Post.* N.p., 25 Feb. 2013. Web. 30 Mar. 2013.

Oreskovic, Alexei. "Facebook Comments, Ads Don't Sway Most Users: Poll." *Reuters.* Thomson Reuters, 04 June 2012. Web. 06 May 2013.

Pink, Daniel H. *A Whole New Mind: Why Right-brainers Will Rule the Future.* New York: Riverhead, 2006. Print.

Pollan, Michael. *In Defense of Food: An Eater's Manifesto.* New York: Penguin, 2008. Print.

Preschool, Wait Until. "When to Introduce Your Child to a Smartphone or Tablet." *PBS.* PBS, n.d. Web. 23 Feb. 2013.

"Professionalism at Work: The Kids Are Not Alright." *At Work RSS.* N.p., n.d. Web. 30 Mar. 2013.

"Proofpoint: Security, Compliance and the Cloud." *Proofpoint: Security, Compliance and the Cloud.* N.p., n.d. Web. 29 Apr. 2013.

Richtel, Matt. "GRADING THE DIGITAL SCHOOL; A Silicon Valley School That Doesn't Compute." *The New York Times.* The New York Times, 23 Oct. 2011. Web. 20 Mar. 2013.

"Rise in Nomophobia: Fear of Being without a Phone." *The Telegraph.* Telegraph Media Group, 28 June 0016. Web. 29 Apr. 2013.

Rogers, Carl R. *On Becoming a Person: A Therapist's View of Psychotherapy.* Boston: Houghton Mifflin, 1989, 1961. Print.

Rosen, Larry. *iDisorder: Understanding Our Obsession with Technology and Overcoming Its Hold on Us.* New York: Palgrave Macmillan, 2012. Print.

Rosenberg, Marshall B. *Nonviolent Communication: A Language of Compassion.* Del Mar, CA: PuddleDancer, 1999. Print.

Sclove, Richard. *Democracy and Technology.* New York: Guilford, 1995. Print.

"Sex and Tech: What's Really Going On." *Sex and Tech.* N.p., n.d. Web. 29 Apr. 2013.

"Sex and Texting." *The National Campaign on Teen Prevention.* N.d. Web.

Siegel, Ronald D. *The Mindfulness Solution: Everyday Practices for Everyday Problems.* New York: Guilford Press, 2010. Print.

Small, Cary, and Gigi Vorgan. *Surviving the Technological Alteration of the Human Mind.* New York: HarperCollins, 2008. Print.

Spechler, Diana. "Health Benefits of Touching - Oprah.com." *Oprah.com.* N.p., n.d. Web. 22 Apr. 2013.

"Statistics About College Depression | World of Psychology." *Psych Central.com.* N.p., n.d. Web. 22 July 2013.

Stuart, Hunter. "Best Buy Ends Work-From-Home Program Known As 'Results Only Work Environment.'" *The Huffington Post.* TheHuffingtonPost.com, 06 Mar. 2013. Web. 30 Mar. 2013.

"Taking Charge of Your Health." *Anxiety & Depression.* N.p., n.d. Web. 24 June 2013.

"Texting Doesn't Replace the Feel-Good Effects of Talking, Study Says." *Texting Doesn't Replace the Feel-Good Effects of Talking, Study Says.* N.p., n.d. Web. 25 May 2013.

"The Sun Magazine | Computing The Cost." *The Sun Magazine | Computing The Cost.* N.p., n.d. Web. 25 Feb. 2013.

"The Touch-Screen Generation." *The Atlantic.* N.p., n.d. Web. 29 Apr. 2013.

"To Facebook You're Worth $80.95." *The CIO Report RSS.* N.p., n.d. Web. 06 May 2013.

Turkle, Sherry. *Alone Together: Why We Expect More from Technology and Less from Each Other.* New York: Basic Books, 2011. Print.

Verderber, Kathleen S., Deanna D. Sellnow and Rudolph F. Verderber. *Comm.* Boston: Wadsworth, 2009. Print.

Wallis, Claudia. "GenM: The Multitasking Generation." *Time.* Time, n.d. Web. 02 May 2013.

Wallis, Claudia. "Time." *Time.* Time, n.d. Web. 18 Feb. 2013.

"Why My iPhone Is Better as a Dumbphone." *Gizmodo.* N.p., n.d. Web. 08 Apr. 2013.

"World Happiness Report." *Columbia Education.* Columbia, 2012. Web.

YCharts. "Who Spends More on Ads -- Apple or Microsoft? Another Lesson in Quality vs Quantity." *Forbes.* Forbes Magazine, 02 Aug. 2012. Web. 06 May 2013.

Made in the USA
Lexington, KY
12 November 2013